# Give Your Child a Head Start In Reading

## by Fitzhugh Dodson

### Illustrations by Al Lowenheim

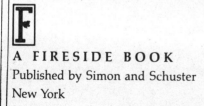

A FIRESIDE BOOK
Published by Simon and Schuster
New York

**Other Books by Fitzhugh Dodson**

How to Parent
How to Father
How to Discipline with Love
I Wish I Had a Computer That Makes Waffles
How to Grandparent

A Fireside Book
Published by Simon and Schuster
A Division of Gulf & Western Corporation
Simon & Schuster Building
Rockefeller Center
1230 Avenue of the Americas
New York, New York 10020
FIRESIDE and colophon are trademarks of Simon & Schuster.
Designed by H. Roberts Design
Manufactured in the United States of America
Printed and bound by The Murray Printing Company
1  2  3  4  5  6  7  8  9  10

Library of Congress Cataloging in Publication Data

Dodson, Fitzhugh, 1923-
    Give your child a head start in reading.

    (A Fireside book)
    Includes bibliographies.
    1. Reading (Preschool) 2. Reading readiness.
3. Domestic education. 4. Children—Books and reading.
I. Title.
LB1140.5.R4D6        372.4        81-14467
ISBN 0-671-43641-4                AACR2

# Contents

# I  The Three Enemies of Reading

I was flying from Los Angeles to give a lecture in Grand Rapids, Michigan, and had a stopover and change of planes in Chicago. During the flight I had been engrossed in a fascinating book by Paul Theroux called *The Old Patagonian Express.*

After I deplaned in Chicago, I hunted down a telephone booth and called my wife. Then I went to the coffee shop to get a snack. I was just finishing up my snack when suddenly the thought hit me, "My book—where is my book?" I looked in my briefcase, but it wasn't there.

"Stupid!" I said to myself. "You must have left it on the plane." I hurried back to Gate 14. The plane was gone. I was mad and disgusted at myself.

Then a heartening thought came to me, "Now wait a minute, Dummy. You had the book in your hand when you got off the plane, so you couldn't have left it there. What have you been doing since you got off the plane? Aha, the telephone call!" I hurried back to the phone booth and discovered my inner voice was right. There was the book, sitting on the ledge inside the booth.

My relief and delight were great, but then I began to mull over the incident. It had been over a half hour since I had left the book there. Yet no one had taken it.

Suppose I had left my wallet for half an hour? Would it have been there when I got back? Obviously not.

Suppose I had left a five-dollar bill? Or even a one-dollar bill? Someone certainly would have swiped it.

Suppose I had left even my ballpoint pen? Someone probably would have made off with it.

And yet I had left this excellent book, worth probably nine or ten dollars, and no one had taken it. Why?

The answer came, clear and strong: *No one steals books in the United States.* Why? Because people don't value books enough to steal them. And the reason they don't value them is that only a minority of Americans likes to read.

The sad truth which this little incident brought home to me is documented more scientifically by a number of research studies.

Dr. George Gallup, for instance, studied a representative sample of adults in the United States. Nearly two-thirds of them said they had not read a single book all the way through during the previous year (excluding the Bible and textbooks). Furthermore, only one adult out of six could think of any recently published book he would especially like to read.[1]

Dr. Gallup commented, "These figures give small comfort to those who defend the present system of education in America."[2] And if we are going to change this unfortunate situation, he continues, "interest in books . . . must be carefully nurtured."[3] That is exactly what I'm going to tell you how to do for your child.

Various other studies show that an enormous number of Americans are either actually illiterate or functionally illiterate. By *actually illiterate* I mean that they cannot read at all. By *functionally illiterate* I mean that they can read to some degree but not enough to function adequately at a job and in society at large.

One study found that 50 percent of the entering students at San Francisco's public two-year college read at a fifth-grade level or below.[4] Another study reported that over a third of the nation's naval recruits read below a tenth-grade level, and 70 percent of these read so poorly they were unable to complete their basic training.[5] A United Press International story tells of a sailor who did a quarter of a million dollars damage to a ship's engines because he could not read the repair manual.[6]

At the University of Texas, researchers studied the illiteracy of Americans by testing thousands of adults with tasks designed to find out if they could function in modern society. The study discovered that about 20 percent of them were functionally incompetent. They could not perform the simplest everyday tasks, such as reading a want ad or a W-2 form, addressing an envelope, or calculating the change due on a purchase. Another 34 percent were found to be barely functioning in these basic skills.[7]

Scientific studies describe the problem of adult illiteracy in an objective, dispassionate way. But I have recently been conducting a semiscientific investigation that has given me a gut-level understanding of the problem.

For the past year I have been asking people a simple question. These are people standing in line with me to buy tickets to shows or sports events, people I meet camping, people I meet on planes or in airports, taxi drivers, clerks at the snack bar in movie theaters when trade is slow, people of all ages and all socioeconomic levels.

I say to them, "I'm a writer. May I ask you a question?" Then I ask, "Over your whole lifetime, what three books that you've read have you liked the best?"

Originally I just wondered what kinds of books people would name, fiction or nonfiction, and whether any particular books would prove to be popular with a lot of people.

I received all kinds of answers, ranging from well-known books such as *Gone With The Wind* to little-known ones such as J. D. Salinger's *Franny and Zooey*. But what bowled me over was the number of people whose answer really boiled down to "I don't read." I'd hear such things as "Well, I've never thought about that before," or "I guess I'm not much of a reader," or "Once I got out of school I didn't go in much for reading," and even "I just don't remember the last time I read a book."

I once asked this question of an acquaintance of mine who is a lawyer. He said, "Listen, I have trouble enough keeping up with my reading in the law to have time to read anything else." Yet I happen to know that this lawyer watches TV, attends football games zealously, and goes fishing as often as he can. Obviously he does these things because he likes to do them. And of course it's good to spend time in recreation that's different from your work. But this man doesn't read *anything* except law books—because he simply doesn't like to read. And the tragedy is, there are millions upon millions like him. The world of books is closed to them.

I'm certain that this lawyer and probably most of the people I've talked to would not think of themselves as functionally illiterate. But they are. They have been taught to read and they know how to, but they don't do it.

How impoverished their lives are! The only information they can take in comes from the TV tube or the radio, or possibly the front page or sports pages of their newspaper. But they will never have the delight of reading Steinbeck or Hemingway, or *Huckleberry Finn* or *Tom Sawyer*, or a modern novel such as James Clavell's *Shōgun*. They cannot benefit from books about deepening a marriage relationship or raising happy and intelligent children. They won't learn from books about the fascinating behavior of people of other countries. They won't read books that describe the newest research into the medical or psychological understanding of human beings. They will never have a chance to learn about philosophy or religion.

In short, for these people, the great thinkers and novelists of all time do not really exist. Because of their non-reading, they are barred forever from the rich knowledge and lore of these writers.

What does all of this mean for you and your child? It means that *chances are approximately fifty-fifty that your child will grow up to be functionally illiterate unless you do something about it.* And the critical years in which you need to do something about it are the first five years of life, before he enters first grade.

Very few parents are aware of the importance of the years *before* school in getting their child ready to learn to read. Most of them do little more preparation than reading him a story now and then. Or perhaps they send him to nursery school and hope that this will prepare him for reading later. Or they may not think in terms of reading readiness at all. They just send him off to school when the time comes, trusting the teachers will teach him whatever he needs to know.

Among the parents who understand the importance of their child's learning to read well, few of them have a planned program for getting him ready to read in first grade. That's what this book offers: a planned program for reading readiness, and a program for helping your child remain an enthusiastic reader throughout the years.

Let's begin by asking this question: What readiness skills will your child need when he is six years old, in order for him to learn to read easily and well? Believe it or not, he will need no less than *twenty-two* different skills!

This is what a child is like who is really ready to learn to read.

1. He can listen carefully and pay attention.
2. He can discriminate among sounds and words that sound alike, but are different.
3. He has a curiosity about words.

4. He can speak words and sentences clearly and correctly.

5. He has a well-developed oral vocabulary.

6. He has a love of language and the cadence of words.

7. He enjoys talking.

8. He has an intense curiosity about the varied information to be found in the world, including the world of books.

9. He has a good imagination.

10. He knows how to think.

11. He can follow directions.

12. He has self-confidence, especially in expressing himself and trying new things.

13. He has had wide experience in many areas, as a background for understanding what he reads.

14. He can visually discriminate letters, especially those that look alike, such as "b" and "d."

15. He uses left-to-right eye movements easily and comfortably.

16. He can recognize and name the capital letters.

17. He can recognize and name the lowercase letters.

18. He can associate the appropriate speech sounds with different letters.

19. He has developed good eye-hand coordination, necessary for printing and writing, which are close allies of reading.

20. He can print the capital letters.

21. He can print the lowercase letters.

22. He is eager to learn how to read.

Does this look like a lot of things for him to learn before he enters first grade? It is. But these skills are all easy for you to teach him. And a number of them go together, so he will learn them at the same time. Some of them he will learn simply by having you talk to him and read to him. The systematic program in this book shows you how to teach all twenty-two skills to your child painlessly and in a fun way. If he enters first grade without them, he can get off to a very bad start in learning to read. He can end up as part of the 50 percent of American adults who are functionally illiterate.

If you would be dismayed at the thought of your child's growing up functionally illiterate, you need to know the three main enemies to combat so that he will grow up to be an adult who reads and enjoys it.

## ENEMY NO. 1. TELEVISION

There is much criticism of television today, from both laymen and professionals. They speak of the banality and stupidity of the programs, the effect of TV violence on children, and the pressure of TV commercials on youngsters to buy junk food, junk toys, and other assorted junk. But this is not what I'm talking about.

Television is Enemy No. 1 of reading on the sheer and simple basis of TIME. John Ruskin said long ago, "If I read this book, I cannot read that book." Today he might say, "If I watch *this* TV show, I cannot read *that* book."

When I was a young boy, I loved to read. I went to the public library at least once a week, and I read voraciously. But when I had the opportunity to go to a movie, there was no contest at all between the book and the movie. I went to the movie. But that was some time ago, and now the entertainment is all free and available at home and we call it television.

Today's children are making basically the same choice I made as a child. They find it more exciting to watch TV than to read books. On any given Saturday (the prime day for TV viewing by children) approximately 75 percent of children in homes with TV will have watched at least one program before the day is over. We are talking about approximately 57 million children.

Preschool children, aged three to five, average fifty-four hours of TV every week. By the time this child of television graduates from high school he will have spent approximately 11,000 hours in school and *more than 22,000 hours in front of a TV set* (and seen at least 250,000 TV commercials).

To any parent who views reading as a precious skill, these figures should be horrifying. For the 22,000 hours of TV watching represents time that was available for reading, but not used.

Sometimes such global figures lose their impact, while a single poignant example brings the message home. So I will give you one. As I write this, my wife and I are camping in a rented camper on the Big Island of Hawaii. I am writing these words on the kitchen table of our camper; my wife is outside, alternating swimming and reading.

Last night a truly mind-boggling thing happened. We were camped at the far end of a beautiful beach park, with coconut trees and surf pounding on lava rocks—a really gorgeous tropical setting. As we were cooking hamburgers over an outdoor fire-pit, another family drove up in a camper. We got acquainted and discovered that they were not tourists, but local people who lived in the nearby city of Hilo. They had four boys, ranging in age from six to twelve. We chatted a bit and then both families finished up their respective dinners.

After dinner my wife and I were sitting on the sea wall, talking and absorbing the beauty of this idyllic spot. It was quiet and peaceful. Suddenly I heard a noise. I thought to myself, It sounds just like a TV, but that can't be! Yes it could. It *was* a TV! The parents had rigged it to run off the generator in their camper, and put it up on top of their picnic table. All of the family, children and adults, were lying around on pillows watching TV. It was about 7 o'clock when they started and they watched till 9:30.

We were stunned. Here was this beautiful beach, and this family had driven fifty miles from Hilo in order to, in the words of the mother, "get away from the rat race in the city." And what do they do when they reach this beautiful spot? They watch TV! Incredible. It's as if this beautiful beach doesn't really exist for them. They could just as well be home in Hilo, gathered together to watch TV in the family room.

After they finished watching TV they all went to bed. I thought about all the things they could have done that evening but didn't. They could have played cards or some game like Monopoly together as a family. They could have gone beach walking or explored tidepools. They could have read, at least part of the time. But you can't read or play cards or talk together or wade in tidepools if you are watching TV.

Somehow, actually seeing this scenario enacted before my eyes got to me as mountains of statistics would not. And I thought to myself, We talk about the menace of drug addiction, of becoming addicted to uppers or downers, speed, LSD, Quaaludes, or heroin. And we think this is the No. 1 dope problem in the United States. But that's not true. The *Number 1 addiction in the United States is TV watching.* We are raising a generation addicted to the most powerful drug in America: the television set. And when children are getting their daily "fix" of TV, they simply can't be reading at the same time. All too many parents, instead of spending time with their children—reading to them or playing or talking together—use TV as an electronic baby-sitter.

Regardless of all the other things about TV that are debated back and forth, one thing cannot be disputed: Time that children could spend reading is preempted by TV watching.

If you agree with my analysis so far, I am sure you are asking yourself, "What can I do about it?" Here are some specific answers.

One way of handling the problem is to take the TV out of the house or forbid the children to watch it altogether.

The main difficulty with this solution is that it makes TV into a Giant Taboo. And whenever you make anything a taboo, particularly for children, all you do is make them even more eager to see it. It's the same as if you said to your child, "You can eat any of the cereals in the pantry except Wheat Chex." Immediately, Wheat Chex becomes the most desirable cereal of all!

So if you forbid your children to watch TV altogether, all you will succeed in doing is to increase fourfold their desire for it. They will then figure out ways to watch it behind your back: when you are away on an errand or are doing yard work outside, or when they are at a friend's house.

Instead of making TV absolutely taboo, I suggest you install Dr. Dodson's Pay-as-You-Go TV in your house. Here's how it works. Suppose you have a six-year-old and a nine-year-old. Make a rough estimate of how many hours per week you want to allow them to watch TV. Let's say arbitrarily you decide to allow a maximum of approximately fifteen hours of TV watching in a seven-day week. Then you decide how much it will cost to watch TV for a half hour. Suppose you decide it will cost a dime.

Then you say to your children something like this. "Jim and Lucy, we've decided to increase your allowance by two dollars and fifty cents a week. (Prolonged applause and cheers) Also, we've decided to start a new system for watching TV. From now on, everybody, both parents and children, has to pay a dime each time he watches a half hour of TV. If the program is an hour long, it costs two dimes. We'll put the money in the kitty and use it for some special treat for the whole family, like a movie, when there's enough of it."

This will immediately change your children's viewing habits. No longer will they sit with glazed eyes all Saturday morning, glued to the tube. No indeed! Since they now have to pay for watching TV they will have to be selective. And that is a bonus in itself. But what is more important, their TV is now limited by the amount of money they are willing to spend on it. So when you compare their TV-watching hours to those of other children their age, your children will have many more hours to spend reading, or playing outdoors, or making crafts, or a host of other creative things they could have been doing before but didn't because they were watching TV instead.

The ideal time to begin the pay-as-you-go system is as soon as your child is old enough to watch TV at all. This way he will take it as an accepted family custom that you each pay to watch television.

But you can do more. You can actually use TV to help your child learn to read or to increase his love of reading. If you have a preschooler, encourage him to watch *Sesame Street* (for ages 2 to 6) or *The Electric Company* (ages 6 to 9). These are two excellent shows that actually teach young children reading skills and they'll love it!

You can use TV with your school-age child too. Check the schedule each week to see if there is a movie or other program based on a book (any readable book, from *Tom Sawyer* to *Charlie and the Chocolate Factory*). Then announce that there is a "free" TV show everybody can watch without having to pay. And you sit down and watch the show with him, unless other duties are too pressing. (You might also offer your preschooler no-pay time for a certain amount of watching of the shows we've recommended, depending on the total number of hours you're willing to have him sitting in front of the set.)

If your older child's interest has been captured by the

movie or show, get him a copy of the book as soon as possible, from the bookstore or the library. You will be using TV as a means of motivating your child to read new books. Whereas much of TV is antireading, you have turned part of your child's TV viewing into proreading.

## ENEMY NO. 2. NONREADING PARENTS.

When we say that approximately 50 percent of the adults in the United States are nonreaders, this includes parents. Consider the effect of nonreading parents on a child. He sees his parents doing many things: watching TV, listening to the car radio, or going swimming or bowling or skiing or playing golf or tennis. But he never sees them reading.

His parents are very interested in *his* learning to read. But believe me, he is very aware of the difference between what his parents say *he* ought to do and what *they themselves* do. The silent message that nonreading parents are sending is, "Reading is not particularly important or fun. If I thought it was, I'd be a reader myself."

In all probability you are not a nonreading parent, or you wouldn't be reading this book now. So this section of the book may not really apply to you. But what about your spouse? In all too many families there is one reading parent and one nonreading one. Of course that's better than having two nonreaders, but it's still not good. Let's say, for example, that the child sees his mother reading from time to time, but not his father. His father is a physician who reads medical books and journals at the office but never reads at home. Or perhaps father is a salesman, and only reads books on salesmanship, never any other books. The parents don't talk with each other about books at the dinner table. Mother may mention a book she is reading, but father does not reciprocate with one he is reading.

This child will come to feel inside: Books are important to mother, but not to father. My dad's a doctor and he's pretty successful without reading. So why do they make such a big thing about it? If Dad doesn't need to do it, why should I? I guess reading must be mostly for women anyway.

One of the most powerful motivators of your children is their desire to imitate their parents, who serve as role models for them. The ideal situation is for them to grow up with a mother and father who are both readers, who love books, and who talk about books to each other and their children. Anything less than this ideal greatly reduces the motivation of your child to want to become a reader, and a good reader, when he grows up. And it greatly reduces his motivation to read books *now*, as a child.

## ENEMY NO. 3. THE SCHOOLS

Yes, as shocking as it may seem to you, *the schools are an enemy of reading!*

By "the schools" I mean approximately 80 percent of both the public and private schools in the United States. Schools are *supposed* to teach reading. But in fact they fail to teach many of our children how to read except very minimally. And they further fail to teach them to love reading. In fact, they teach them to *hate* it.

Let's get down to cases. We'll begin in the first grade. It is certainly true that many first-grade teachers *think* they are teaching reading. But instead, in many of those classrooms, the children are only learning to memorize words by the look-and-say method (I prefer to call it the look-and-guess method).

Children who are taught to read by the look-and-say method are made to memorize the configuration of the whole word. So if a child can read a thousand words, this means she has had to memorize a thousand different configurations. In my opinion it would be difficult to invent a more inefficient and exasperating way of teaching a child to read.

But memorizing words is not the same as reading. A language is a code. The English language is a code with twenty-six letters and approximately forty-four sounds. When you teach a child to read, you teach her how to crack the code, and there is only one way to do that. You teach the sound or sounds of each letter. In a 100 percent phonetic language such as Spanish, there is only one sound for each of the twenty-six letters. English is approximately 87 percent phonetic, and the other 13 percent is irregular.

Even though English is not as easy to teach as Spanish, you begin by teaching the phonic sounds of the letters that are regular. Then you move on to the letter sounds that are irregular. Once your child has learned the basic phonic rules and the exceptions to the rules, she can sound out any word in the English language. In other words, she can read any book in English, even though the reading level of the book might make it difficult for her to comprehend easily.

The basic reason so many children fail to learn to read well in first grade is that instead of being taught to sound out letters and syllables, they have memorized perhaps 450 words and have read a succession of dull, dull books based only on those words. Books that contain sentences such as "The cat sat on the floor. The cat sat on the chair. The cat sat on the pillow. The cat ate his food."

If you give these children a book with a sentence in it such as "I saw a kangaroo," they are lost. All they can do is to guess wildly. They will say such things as "I saw a king" or "I saw a kitty-cat." Can you imagine how frustrating it is for a young child, eager to learn the magic process of reading, to be totally unable to figure out the words in a new book?

Think how formidable the English language seems to six-year-old children who are learning it by memorizing words. Imagine yourself memorizing 10,000 words, or 20,000 or 30,000. Doesn't the idea make you shudder?

With the phonics method, when a child sounds out a new word in class and the pronunciation is not correct, the teacher tells her, and also explains what the word means. So she is rewarded by being told the meaning of the new word. If it's one that is not already in her oral vocabulary, such as "didactic" or "maelstrom," then the teacher will need to elaborate on the meaning. There is no need for wild guessing. And a word that the child has learned by sounding it out will begin to soak into her memory faster.

Reading and writing and spelling all belong together and should be taught together. But in schools where students are taught word-guessing instead of reading, they are not taught writing at all. And they are taught spelling as a separate subject all its own, by the memorization of whole words. A more inefficient way of teaching spelling would be hard to imagine.

What should happen is that your child learns to write and read and spell at the same time, using the phonics method. That is, she is taught one letter symbol at a time, and she learns how to write it and how to recognize it and how to sound it out. By the time the teacher has piloted her through the whole list of letter symbols, she can read and write. And although spelling is technically a separate subject, it is taught phonetically and is an integral part of the reading and writing process. It is then only a matter of time and practice for your child to learn to read faster and more automatically.

I want to call your attention to something very important about children. Babies all over the world babble, and their babbling sounds are pretty much the same. But by the time they get to be two or two and a half, they have all learned to speak the language of the country in which they have been raised, whether it's Spanish or Chinese or Japanese or Russian or Greek or English or German. That is an incredible intellectual feat. What is more incredible is the fact that *nobody taught them to speak the language.* They learned it by absorbing the words and sentences they heard spoken around them. They learned it not by memorizing words but by figuring out the structure of the language, *all by themselves.* And if you know any languages you will know how different Chinese and Spanish are, and German with all its words piled up in the sentence and the verb at the end, and English with its basic subject-verb-object structure. Still, the children learn.

Now my question is this. If little kids are so smart that they can figure out the structure of very complex languages, why do we have so many reading problems in American schools and so many nonreaders in America? Are our children brilliant between the ages of nine months and two years, and do they then suddenly become stupid when they enter the door of their schoolhouse at age six? Obviously not.

In my analysis of how children learn to read and what gets in the way of it, I find myself exactly where Dr. Rudolph Flesch ended up in his 1955 nook, *Why Johnny Can't Read:* "The teaching of reading is too important to be left to the educators." [8]

Flesch goes on to say:

> The teaching of reading all over the United States, in all the schools, in all the textbooks—is totally wrong and flies in the face of all knowledge and common sense. Johnny (a 12-year-old boy whom Dr. Flesch worked with on an individual basis to teach him to read) couldn't read until

half a year ago for the simple reason that nobody had
showed him how. Johnny's only problem was that he was
unfortunately exposed to an ordinary American school.[9]

Dr. Flesch's book, although it had quite an impact on
parents, did not cause an immediate substitution of phonics for word-guessing in the schools. Educators did get
bristly and defensive when his book was mentioned, but it
certainly didn't cause any revolution in the schools.

But 1966 saw the publication, of *Learning to Read: The
Great Debate*, by Dr. Jeanne Chall of Harvard. Dr. Chall
spent ten years studying the results of all the research done
(from 1912 to 1965) on teaching reading by both look-and-
say and a variety of phonics methods. She states that the
research indicates that any phonics method produces better results than look-and-say in teaching beginning reading. No phonics method was superior to any other phonics
method; but *every* phonics method was superior to look-
and-say. Dr. Chall adds that the phonics results are better
not merely in terms of the mechanical aspects of literacy,
but also in terms of the ultimate goals of reading instruction: comprehension and possibly even speed of reading.

You would assume that after publication of these
impressive results in Dr. Chall's scholarly work, all the
schools in America would immediately switch from look-
and-guess to phonics. That did not happen. What did happen is that a lot of schools started paying lip service to
phonics.

This is what I mean. When a parent who has heard
about what phonics does in comparison to look-and-guess
goes to school to find out how her Jennifer is being taught
reading, this is what she is likely to hear: "Oh, dear, Mrs.
Jones, you bet your boots we use phonics in our reading
program. You don't have to worry about that. We believe
in phonics."

But the administrators and reading teachers usually do

not mean the same thing by the word *phonics* as I mean (and Dr. Chall meant). I mean a complete systematic program for the first year or two years in school, in which the child thoroughly masters the language code and learns to read. She can sound out any word in any book. And in the rest of her schooling she will simply learn to read faster and with more comprehension.

That's what I mean by *phonics*. But what educators often mean is *phonics* as one factor out of maybe ten other factors in the teaching of reading, a very unsystematic program.

When a slapdash unsystematic approach that gives only a surface knowledge of phonics is palmed off as thorough and systematic, it is hard for a parent to tell. The only way to tell is to spend a few weeks sitting in a classroom finding out how Jennifer is *really* being taught to read.

Not only do the schools teach reading badly, they systematically teach your child to hate reading, finishing off the process in her senior year of high school. Of course, English teachers believe exactly the reverse. The believe they are teaching young people a love of reading and of good literature. But let's see.

When you and I as adults begin to read a book, any book, and find that it is dull and boring or for some reason does not appeal to us, what do we do? We stop reading it.

For example, many people have told me that Tolstoy's *War and Peace* is one of the world's greatest novels. I have tried to read it three separate times, beginning in college, but I have never been able to get farther than 100 pages in it. I simply found it too boring; it never managed to catch my interest.

On a completely different level, I once tried to read Jacqueline Susann's *Valley of the Dolls*. I was never able to get farther than thirty pages in that one, and I never tried again.

On the other hand, here are some books, varying a

great deal in subject matter and writing style, that I have read at least four times and some as many as twelve times: Mark Twain's *Huckleberry Finn*, John Steinbeck's *The Grapes of Wrath* and *Tortilla Flat*, James Michener's *Hawaii*, Frederick Forsyth's *The Day of the Jackal*, B. Traven's *The Treasure of Sierra Madre*, and Howard Spring's *Fame Is the Spur*.

If you are a reading adult, I can only assume that you operate on the same principle that I do. You read the books that you enjoy reading, and you do not continue to read books that bore or repel you.

Unfortunately the schools do not operate so sensibly. They use what I call the "Silas Marner principle." I cannot remember what grade I was in when I was forced to read that book and write a report on it. I only remember that I (and most of my classmates) detested it thoroughly. Our English teacher assured our class it was "great literature," but if I had written an honest report on it, it would have been one sentence long: "I hated reading this book."

Here is a current example of the Silas Marner principle in action. A few months ago my wife and I went to the movies. It was a small neighborhood theater in the middle of the week with no line. I noticed that the girl at the ticket counter, who was of high school age, was writing on a thick paper tablet which she had propped up on her lap. I asked her jokingly, "A letter to your boyfriend, or are you writing a novel?" "Neither," she answered, "I'm writing a report on this stupid book" and she held up a book by John Cheever.

"Why are you reading the book if you think it's stupid?" I asked.

"Because I have to. The whole class has to read the dumb book."

It certainly doesn't take a giant intellect to figure out that if this girl is forced to read books she dislikes, year after year after year, it does not exactly help her develop a love of reading.

Anyone with an elementary knowledge of psychology should realize that it is a mistake to have all the members of a class read the same book, because it would be an extraordinary thing for the members of any class to find that the same book appeals to all of them. Each child is a unique personality, with reading likes and dislikes that are not shared 100 percent or maybe not even 15 percent by the other children.

The remedy for this situation is simple, although the schools have not discovered it yet. *Let each child read whatever books she wants to, as long as she is reading.* You may say, "But the schools are already doing that! They let children read the books that interest them." No they don't. They put out a list of books, and the children choose the books to read *from that list.* That is by no means the same as letting the children choose the books that they really want to read.

To help you understand how it feels when you are compelled to read something that is over your head or that doesn't appeal to you, I'm going to give you, as an adult, a list of books to choose from. To simplify things a bit, I'm going to make it a very short list of only two books: *Interdisciplinary Phenomenology: Selected Studies in Phenomenology and Existential Philosophy,* by Richard Zaner and Don Ihde; and *The Great Philosophers,* by Karl Jaspers. To save you going to the library, I'm reprinting this paragraph from *Phenomenology and Existentialism:*

> The unique thought that *Sein und Zeit* attempts to express, wants to achieve, is something simple. As such, Being remains mysterious, the plain closeness of an unobtrusive task. This closeness is essentially language itself. Yet the language is not merely language, insofar as we imagine it at the most as the unity of sound-form (script), melody and rhythm and meaning. We think of sound-form and script as the body of the word: of melody and rhythm as the soul and meaning as the mind of language. We

generally think of language as corresponding to the essence of man, insofar as this essence is represented as *animal rationale*, i.e., as the unity of body-soul-mind. But as in the *humanitas* of the *homo animalis* ex-sistence remains concealed and through this the relation of the truth of Being to man, so does the metaphysical-animal interpretation of language conceal its essence from the point of view of the history of Being.[10]

How did you like it? Would you like to read all 374 pages of it? You wouldn't? What a surprise! Well, maybe you'll like *The Great Philosophers* better. Here's a nice easy paragraph from it:

> In order to become more conscious of what we can know in the modes of thought through which being is for us, we must distinguish between our existence insofar as we know and those things which cannot be objects of our cognition. While in our existence our consciousness as such distinguishes one existent from another and we deal with contents, the total content of consciousness as such can be distinguished only from something that is not accessible to our understanding. After Kant has marked off the limits of our possible knowledge, there remains, outside them, what he calls the "thing in itself," the intelligible or noumenal world. Our understanding does not tell us whether it is possible.[11]

How does that one grab you? Can you think of anything more thrilling than settling down with a cup of coffee or a cool drink for an afternoon of undisturbed reading?

Now imagine I have thirty other books pretty much like those two, and I give you free choice. You can pick whatever book you want out of my list to read and write a report on. I'll bet you wouldn't like to do this any more than children do.

All of this mental anguish can be avoided if the schools would really, and I mean *really*, let the students pick out their own books. The teachers can put out a list they think would interest a student in that grade level, but the student should have the freedom, if she doesn't like *any* of the books on the list, to find her own.

If you are interested in reading more about this particular subject, I would recommend *Hooked on Books*, by Dr. Daniel Fader. He worked with two groups of teenagers who hated reading (black students at an inner-city high school in Detroit and teenagers in a juvenile detention center). The book tells how he gradually taught them to love reading, using what I call the Pick Up and Put Down Principle. The student can pick up any book that looks interesting. But she can put it down if she doesn't like it and pick up another one. Then when she finds one she likes, she will read it.

As a concerned parent, you may wish to dig deeper into the subject of the failure of the schools to teach reading adequately. I suggest you read two books: *Why Johnny Can't Read*, by Rudolph Flesch; and *The Literary Hoax*, by Paul Kopperman.

As I write these words I am sitting in my camper, typing at the kitchen table. I happen to glance across at the paperback book *Day of the Jackal*, which I am in the middle of reading for the fourth time. I find that I enjoy it as much each time I reread it. My wife just finished James Michener's *Hawaii* two days ago, which she had never read before. And as I think of the ways in which schools effectively teach children not to read and enjoy books like *Hawaii* or *Day of the Jackal* or any books, a feeling of sadness comes over me.

Children are being robbed of the priceless gift of books and of reading. And robbed by the very institution that should teach them to love and cherish reading! I know you don't want this to happen to your children. And in the next section I am going to tell you, step-by-step, what you can do to help your child to grow up to love reading. And you will do this at home, in the first five years of her life, before she gets to first grade.

When your child begins first grade, she will have benefited enormously from the reading-readiness skills you have taught her. Reading, writing, and spelling should come easily for her in school. She won't encounter the obstacles that block other children's progress from the start. And the entire first year of school (which is centered on reading) will be the most positive experience possible for her.

As a parent, don't you want to put those first five years, when your child is yours alone, to the best possible use?

# II  A Preschool Reading-Readiness Program

## YOU READ WITH YOUR BRAIN

Which part of your body do you read with?

Your eyes, of course—right? Wrong. You read with your brain.

It is not our eyes alone that do the reading. Here is proof that our eyes only transmit the word images to the brain, which then interprets them. In a book I was recently reading, this sentence appeared: "He was quiet opposed to it." Think for a minute about the person who was the copy editor for this book. His job is to correct all errors of spelling, punctuation, and grammar. His eyes sent the message to his brain that the third word in the sentence was *quiet*. But his brain "read" the word as *quite*. That's why the mistake went unnoticed. If his brain had correctly read *quiet*, he would have caught the error and it would not have appeared in the book. (But don't be too hard on the poor copy editor. Perhaps he was taught to read by look-and-guess.)

Your brain is like a computer. When you read, it uses its vast information-storage center to tuck away such things as: the words you know when you hear them spoken (your oral vocabulary); the words you know when you see them in print (your written vocabulary); all the feeling-tones you have about reading ("I hate reading" or "I love to read"); your self-confidence about trying new things (("I don't think I'll be able to handle something new" or "I'm a good reader and I'll be able to handle a new book, even though I may have to use the dictionary and puzzle over some sentences"). All these words, bits of information, feelings, and attitudes play a part in how fast and how efficiently your brain decodes the messages that your eyes send.

The important thing to remember is this: *When your child goes to first grade, the amount of information already in his brain will be largely determined by the kind of reading-readiness skills you provided for him in the first five years of life.*

It is your child's brain, not his eyes, that controls his verbal ability. By verbal ability I mean such things as recognizing sounds and words by ear; enjoying "playing around" with sounds and making up nonsense words; being curious about the words on cereal packages, signs, and cartoons; understanding the meaning of spoken sentences; and speaking words and sentences clearly and correctly. These are the kinds of verbal abilities your child develops in his first five years of life before he enters school. And you, his parent, are his main teacher in helping him develop strong verbal interests and skills.

As Dr. Nancy Larrick, one of our foremost authorities on children's reading and literature puts it, "Parents are the major influence in a child's development as a reader. At school he can build on the foundation he has gotten at home. Without that foundation he will probably have a struggle." [12]

The program to help you get your child ready to read

can be roughly divided into four stages: babyhood (birth to walking); toddlerhood (walking to two years); first adolescence (two years to three); and preschool (three years to six).

## BABYHOOD

You can begin helping your baby build his foundation for reading as soon as he is born. For learning to read really begins with a baby's first conversation with another person: you. Talk to your baby! When you're feeding him you can say, "Isn't that milk good? Tastes great, huh? And doesn't it feel wonderful to snuggle up against Mommy when you nurse?" Talk to him when you change his diapers: "Okay, kid, off with the old dirty diapers and on with the fresh ones—here we go!" Talk to him when you bathe him, "Doesn't that water feel wonderful? Isn't that a great and glorious feeling? You know it is." Talk to him anytime at all about anything at all, "Hey, do you know you're my absolutely favorite baby and I love you?" Or "Baby boy, I've got to tell you the sad news; we may as well face it together, kid—the Dodgers lost today." And don't limit yourself to just talking to him. Sing to him. What can you sing? Anything and everything. My favorite songs I sang to my kids when they were babies were *The Erie Canal* and *The Eyes of Texas.*

Of course your baby won't understand what you're saying, but don't think that you are wasting your breath. Far from it. Your baby is learning the sounds of letters and words and hearing how sentences are put together, and he's filing away the sounds in his computer storage box. So these first "conversations" with your baby are providing him with an auditory environment of words and sentences that form the foundation for his verbal skills.

Please don't interpret this to mean that you should be jabbering away at your baby every second he is awake, drowning him in a sea of words. Don't be like the patient whose doctor prescribed two pills a day to cure an illness. The patient took sixteen, figuring if two pills were good, sixteen would be eight times as effective. Just talk to your baby naturally and normally at various times of the day as you feel like it.

Another thing you can do to provide a good oral language environment for your baby is to play him ethnic music records and tapes. By this I mean music from many different cultures: Africa, Tahiti, Hawaii, Greece, Italy, Mexico, Spain, Japan, China, Russia, and the United States. The great variety of tempo, rhythm, melody, and instrumentation of the different records compels the baby to pay attention to the music in a way he would not if you simply played the music of a single country.

These records teach your baby that his environment contains lots of interesting and fascinating sounds. Since these new sounds captivate him, they give him painless lessons in the skill of paying attention. Children are not born with the ability to pay attention to sounds; it is something they have to learn. And when he is learning to read in first grade, he will need to be able to hear the differences in sounds, or there'll be a giant roadblock in the way of his learning to read. But these ethnic records will help your baby to become fascinated by sounds, to enjoy them, and to distinguish them.

I have listed a group of excellent music records of different cultures, in Appendix A. You probably won't be able to find them (or even similar ones) in your local record shop or the music center of your department store, even if you live in a big city. But you can buy them by mail from a store in Santa Monica, California, that specializes in children's records. Incidentally, they also sell children's books by mail, and it would be wise for you to send for their free catalog of both records and books. This store is: Children's Book and Music Center, 2400 Santa Monica Boulevard, Santa Monica, CA 90404.

By the way, should your baby start crying or show any fear or distress when you play one of these records (although it's unlikely), turn the record off immediately. Try it again a day or so later with the volume down. You certainly don't want to force your baby to listen to music that he finds displeasing.

An infant is very much aware of sound. Although he seems to be passive as he lies there awake in his crib, he is actively exploring his visual environment with his eyes and his aural environment with his ears. The famous Swiss psychologist Jean Piaget has said, "The more a child sees, the more he wants to see; the more a child hears, the more he wants to hear." Your "conversations" with your baby and the music you play will help to give him the varied and stimulating auditory environment that he needs to build a love of language.

And, dear Mother, don't forget about your husband in this program of enrichment for your baby. It is a sad fact of family life that fathers are typically not particularly involved with their babies and young children. One study reported that a representative sample of middle-class fathers spent approximately thirty-seven seconds per day in one-to-one interaction with their year-old children! Try to prevent your husband from being part of a statistic like that. He may not be fully aware that what goes into his baby's brain from birth to age six will have a great deal to do with how successful his child will be in learning to read in first grade. See if you can get your husband to read this book, so that he will have an awareness of his importance in helping to develop language skills. Perhaps then he will willingly join you in the delightful task of talking to your baby and playing records for him.

Your communications with your child will be one

sided at first. But by the beginning of the second month, you may find him beginning to respond with his form of talking: gurgles and coos. By the time he is eight months old (or perhaps earlier), he will be responding to your conversation by saying to you brightly, "Shoberje spish?" Then he is entering a new and enchanting phase of his oral language development. For when he says, "Shoberje spish" to you, you can repeat "Shoberje spish" back to him.

When you respond to him this way, you are teaching him that language is not only something people do by themselves, but also something they do together. Second, you are teaching him that he can have an effect on his environment. For when he says "Shoberje spish," lo and behold you say "Shoberje spish" right back! This is psychologically very rewarding to him. He is thrilled to discover that he can cause his environment to respond to him.

This phase of language development is usually a delightful one for parents. The jargon words of their baby begin to sound like a wondrous language from outer space, with words and sentences and mysterious meanings all its own. The inflections and cadences are there, but the words can be understood only by a genuine space dweller.

Incidentally, I want to make sure no one misunderstands me. When your baby starts speaking jargon and you repeat it back, I don't mean to imply that you should confine your conversation to this gibberish. Of course you will continue to converse with him in normal speech also.

There is another aspect of your child's mental and emotional growth during babyhood that influences his reading readiness greatly. This is his self-concept and his self-confidence.

Your child's self-concept is like a mental map he has of himself. We grownups each have a well-developed mental map of this kind. You, for example, might feel that you are good at mathematics but not so hot at public speaking. You also have definite feelings about things you like and dislike doing, the kind of people you feel comfortable with, and so forth.

Your child begins to form this kind of map of himself when he is born, and he continues to fill it in throughout his life. In each stage of development, as he masters a new psychological task, his self-concept is being formed.

In babyhood your child learns either basic trust of himself and the world, or basic distrust, or something in between. This is how he learns trust: if he is fed on self-demand rather than a rigid schedule (that is, if he is fed when he is hungry); if he receives lots of physical cuddling (which is the only way he has of knowing he is loved); and if his routine needs are taken care of (such as having baths, being comforted when he cries, having his diapers changed, etc.). When all these things are done for the baby in a fairly consistent way, he will come to feel: "This is a wonderful world I live in, one I can trust. When I'm hungry, I get fed. When my diapers are wet and uncomfortable, somebody dries and powders me and gives me fresh ones. When I feel lonely and need love, somebody cuddles me." When a baby learns to feel this kind of trust in the world, he has taken his very first step toward developing the self-confidence that he will need to tackle new tasks, such as learning to read. And he will have taken many more steps in this direction by the time he enters school.

Many parents think of learning to read as purely an intellectual happening; they overlook its emotional aspects. Imagine that you were learning to walk a tightrope eighty feet in the air in a circus. And you were going to be doing it for the first time. How would you feel? You might feel very secure because you have lots of self-confidence in general and have already done similar things. Or you might be mildly scared. Or terribly scared.

Your youngster's learning to read is similar to your learning to walk the tightrope. If he believes that he has the ability to tackle new things and master them, and if you have helped him to feel at home in the world of books, it will be a big help to him in learning to read. So you see, we learn to read with our emotions as well as with our intellect.

Your baby will be ready to take a major step in language development when he is approximately nine months old. Then you can begin to play what I call the Label the Environment game with him. When you are giving him a bath, hold up the piece of soap and say "soap." Ruffle the water with your hands or pour a handful of water over him and say "water." When you are feeding him a banana, say "banana."

At first he will be a passive recipient of your instruction. You will point to the object or person and say the word, but he will be silent or perhaps say "prosh." But sooner or later (and the time will vary enormously with different babies), you will point to the soap and say "soap," and he will respond, "soap." Still later you will be able to point to the soap and say "What's this?" and he will answer "soap."

In playing Label the Environment, don't try to pressure your baby past his interest point. If he tells you by body language that he is bored or uninterested in playing the game any further, drop it and turn to something else. Pressure won't help him to love learning.

## TODDLERHOOD

When your baby begins to crawl and walk, he enters the stage of toddlerhood which lasts until approximately his second birthday. During this stage he is faced with his next task of psychological development, which builds on the basic trust he has learned as a baby. This next task is to learn self-confidence (or self-doubt) in his world. Toddler-hood is the age of exploration, and your young explorer wants to discover everything he can about his world—every shelf, every tabletop, every cupboard, every room, every open door. If he is surrounded by a thousand no-no's and prevented from this psychologically important exploration, he will develop feelings of self-doubt about venturing forth into new areas. But if he is allowed to explore freely in a safe and child-proofed house, then he will develop feelings of self-confidence that add to his good self-concept.

During this stage you can continue playing Label the Environment with your child, and your verbal relationship will become much richer and more complex. Your child will begin to talk as he plays in his sandbox or with his toys in the living room. You can join in his talk at appropri-ate times. "You like the way the sand runs through your fingers, don't you?" or "It's fun to play with your dolls and your cars."

Now you can also start playing Label the Environment in the form of books. For this you need such books as Richard Scarry's *Best Word Book Ever*, as well as other Richard Scarry books. *Best Word Book Ever* contains 1,400 people and objects and the 1,400 words that label them. *The Cat in the Hat Picture Dictionary* by Dr. Seuss is another excellent book of people and objects. You can also use things that people ordinarily do not think of as books, such as catalogs from Sears or Montgomery Ward.

With books, you play the Label the Environment game the same way as before. You point to the automobile and say, "automobile." At first the child will usually say nothing. Then later on you can point to the automobile and say, "What's this?" If he says "automobile," praise him and say, "Very good, Jacob, that's an automobile." If he can't get it yet, simply say, "That's an automobile." and go on to the next one.

Later, your child will proudly show you that he can

now identify many of the objects and people. He will point to the automobile and say, "That's an automobile."

When your child is about one and a half, you can begin to read nursery rhymes to him. For many years, nursery rhymes have been the first oral language learning games for children. There are several ways in which they are special in fostering verbal skills.

Nursery rhymes are sentences set to music. They are written on an intellectual level that a very young child can understand. And because of the rhythm and cadence of the rhymes, they are more interesting to a child than flat prose. Also, they are easier than prose to learn and remember. A child likes to participate in the reading of nursery rhymes. He will join with you in patting his hands together as you read, "pat-a-cake, pat-a-cake, baker's man," or rub his hands together as you read, "rub-a-dub-dub, three men in a tub." These rhymes are short enough for the limited attention span of the very young child.

Your child will enjoy hearing some of these traditional Mother Goose rhymes. But unfortunately, the background and vocabulary of many others are outdated for today's children. "Little Miss Muffet sat on a tuffet, eating her curds and whey." What's a tuffet? What are curds and whey? I'll bet you don't know. Most adults don't. You can look up such words in the dictionary and explain them to your child, if you like. Perhaps he will learn something about cows and milk and farm life. But the old-fashioned world of Mother Goose is difficult for today's child to relate to.

The fascinating environment of today's young child consists of airplanes, libraries, computers, space capsules, electric razors, nursery schools, working mothers, TV, astronauts, and many other things that simply did not exist at the time the Mother Goose rhymes were written. Young children today need nursery rhymes that are modern, that reflect today's environment—the world *they* live in.

A more important consideration as far as Mother Goose rhymes are concerned is that a number of them are sexist. Take "Peter, Peter Pumpkin Eater," for example.

Peter, Peter
Pumpkin Eater;
Had a wife
And couldn't keep her.

(Sounds as if he regards his wife somewhat as a pet raccoon.)

Put her in a pumpkin shell
And there he kept her very well.

(He claps her into the pumpkin shell, slams down the lid, and there she is, silent and submissive, just the way the wife of a male chauvinist pumpkin eater should be!) When we talk about the words and concepts a child learns at the ages of one and a half to two, we are talking about the very earliest level of conceptual learning; and it is therefore especially important. You certainly don't want to teach *either* your son or daughter a sexist way of viewing male-female relationships, particularly at such an important and tender age.

My solution to these difficulties with Mother Goose is to eliminate the rhymes that are unsuitable and read only the others. For example, two that I like are "Hickory Dickory Dock" and "Jack Be Nimble, Jack Be Quick."

Up until a few years ago, parents had only the Mother Goose book to choose nursery rhymes from. But now there are two books of modern nursery rhymes, tailor made for today's children. They are nonsexist, and attuned to the contemporary world. I must confess I am biased in favor of these two books, because I wrote them.

The first of the books is *I Wish I Had a Computer That Makes Waffles*. The second book is the one you are holding in your hands. For the last part of this book is "I Wish I Had a Computer That Makes Ice Cream Cones." It contains thirty-eight new nursery rhymes that are modern, nonsexist, and educational. The verses in both books will delight your child.

When you read him the rhymes, sit him on your lap. Let the reading be a close, warm experience. Point out different things in the pictures that go with the verses. Don't try to get him to memorize the rhymes. Simply continue reading them over and over to him and you will find sooner or later that he will know them by heart. You can also play little games with him in which you read a line and leave a word out and see if he can fill it in.

You can use both Mother Goose rhymes and my modern verses with your child in the course of normal, daily activities. For example, when you are giving your child a bath you can recite this bathtub rhyme from *I Wish I Had a Computer That Makes Waffles:*

The ship is taking
A bath in the sea;
My soap is taking
A bath with me.[13]

You'll soon find that you can recite many of the poems from memory yourself. This lends them a nice feeling of flowing naturally from you, and it lets you have both hands free to bathe or feed or dress your child.

You can use all three of these books of rhymes up until the time your child is six or seven and has outgrown them. He will outgrow them in the sense that he doesn't clamor for you to read them to him anymore. But he will never outgrow the effect your reading them has had on his life. Nursery rhymes that he has heard again and again and knows by heart will have helped him to be fascinated and intrigued by words and rhymes at an early age. They will have exerted a powerful effect on the development of his oral language.

It is safe to say that there are millions of children who are *not* fascinated and intrigued by words or by language. These are the children who are the nonreaders—or children who can read but choose not to. They never pick up a book in preference to turning on a TV program. They reveal their lack of curiosity about words by their sloppy use of words, their poor writing, and their atrocious spelling. And as for reading poetry, they would just as soon do an extra week's homework assignment.

These are the children who were exposed too late (or not at all) to the magic of words and the music of language. So when you read nursery rhymes to your child beginning at one and a half, when you talk to him, when you say words to him, you are teaching him to love words and language very early in life. And that is the right time to do it.

# FIRST ADOLESCENCE

Your child next comes to the stage of what we call first adolescence, which lasts from approximately the second to approximately the third birthday. This may be a difficult stage in which to teach him things that will aid his language development. In the stages of infancy and toddler-hood, he was eager and receptive to being taught. But first adolescence is different. This is characteristically a rebellious stage, and he may resist your efforts to teach him or play games with him.

If you are not already familiar with the characteristics of this age, it might be helpful for me to give you a brief thumbnail personality sketch.

Some people call this stage from two to three the "terrible two's." Although this description is accurate with respect to surface behavior, it does not tell us what is going on *inside* the child. I prefer the term *first adolescence*, because of this stage's great similarity to *second adolescence*—the teenage years. Both first and second adolescence are transitional stages, one from babyhood to true childhood, the other from childhood to adulthood. There is always a lot of anxiety and rebellious behavior in a transitional stage, and first adolescence certainly demonstrates that.

Your child tends to be rigid and inflexible. He wants what he wants when he wants it, and he wants it NOW! It is very difficult for him to compromise, to give a little, to adapt to the wishes of another person.

He acts like the Little King, the ruler of the house. He is domineering and demanding and loves to give orders. This is a stage of violent emotions, with frequent changes of mood. It is often hard to introduce new things to him, such as new foods or new clothes. His favorite word is NO! This is why he may resist your teaching him at this stage, although he has gone along with it happily at the earlier stage of toddlerhood. He will be open and cooperative once again in the preschool stage (when he reaches three).

He likes rituals. Everything must be done in just a certain way and with a certain routine. He is famous for his rigidity. And of course, a rigid personality stance is not the best condition in which to teach him anything, including reading-readiness skills. At this age he will often make strong demands on your patience.

On the other hand, a child at this age is usually vigorous, enthusiastic, and energetic. He can even be charming at times, with his exuberance, his imaginativeness, his enthusiastic zest for life, and his sense of wonder at the new and unspoiled world he sees. So at unexpected times he may be receptive to your teaching.

Please try not to be discouraged if you find your child difficult to cope with, let alone to teach. This stage will pass in about a year.

Even though your two-year-old may be resistant to your teaching, he has matured a great deal and is now much more capable of understanding what you have to teach him about language. Continue to read nursery rhymes to him and weave them into the day's activities. This will further develop his maturing oral language skills. For written language, continue reading Richard Scarry's *Best Word Book Ever*, as well as other Richard Scarry books, and *The Cat in the Hat Picture Dictionary*.

By now your child is ready for somewhat more sophisticated books than those that merely have a picture of a person or object with a word attached to it. He is now ready for a book with a continuous story, although it needs to be a short one. His attention span is still not very long. The kind of book a child of this age likes is *Goodnight Moon*, by Margaret Wise Brown. It takes about ten minutes to read. Your child may like to talk with you about the story while you are reading it, or afterward. You will find a list of other books for the first-adolescent child in Appendix B of this book.

Continue playing Label the Environment with your child. And now, when he is two, the game can begin to take on a new meaning for him. For now you can tell him something that will bring together in one statement all the innumerable times you have played this game. You can say, "Thomas, everything in the world has a name. And it's lots of fun to find out the names of all the different things in the world." Once your child understands the meaning of this statement, it should have the same powerful effect on developing his command of oral language as it did on blind, deaf, and dumb Helen Keller, when her teacher

Anne Sullivan finally was able to get her to understand that everything has a name.

You can also demonstrate this concept visually to your child. Begin with his own name. Tell him, "Thomas, I'm going to print your name." Have ready a piece of brightly colored typing paper, such as yellow or pink, and print his name in both capital and lowercase letters like this: Thomas. Then cut around the name and make a sign to scotch-tape to the door of his room. Make it a special ceremony and give him ice cream or some other treat that he likes.

After you have printed his name, ask him to tell you what is the next thing in the house that he wants you to print the name of. Let's assume the next thing is "trike." Print it the right size to scotch-tape on his trike. Print and tape the names of as many objects as he wants. Don't do anything else special with the names; just leave them taped to the objects for a few days.

It's important to note that you are *not* trying to teach these words to your child. If he should happen to learn the word on his own, or figure out how to spell the word, that's perfectly okay. But don't try to teach him! Your purpose in taping these words to different objects in the house is simply to awaken his curiosity to written words, and to teach him in a different way: "Everything has a name."

The least that can come from this is that naming things in the home will pique your child's curiosity about the mystery of words and of reading. The most that can happen is that he will add these words to his sight vocabulary before he even learns to read, just as he learns to recognize the names on cereal boxes, stop signs, and "in" and "out" signs in stores.

At the same time, you can begin to expand your conversations with your child. At times when he seems in a mood to cooperate, you can ask him simple questions, such as, "These two leaves are different, aren't they? Can you show me how they're different?" Try to avoid closed-end questions, which can only be answered by "yes" and "no." Instead, use open-end questions, which have no one fixed answer and which he can expand on more fully.

There is one final thing you can do for your youngster, even at this somewhat difficult age. You can provide him with the largest blackboard you can find (a four-by-four would be nice). "What's the use of a blackboard at this age?" you may say. "He'll just scribble on it!" You're probably right, but you underestimate the educational importance of that primitive scribbling of his.

In order to learn to print and later to write, he will need to develop the finger-thumb small-muscle coordination which is basic to both of these activities. How does he do that? By scribbling! So scribbling is not a foolish activity or a waste of time; it is a necessary preparation for learning to print and write. He can draw on the blackboard with either white or colored chalk. The blackboard also affords an outlet for his urge to scribble, so he will be less apt to use the walls of your house for his art work.

The same blackboard he uses to scribble on at age two he will use to print on at ages three and four and five—and perhaps to do cursive writing on after that.

## THE PRESCHOOLER

Your child next enters the preschool stage, which runs from approximately her third birthday to her sixth. As she reaches three you will find she is becoming more easygoing again, and much more amenable to your teaching. The years from three to six are an extraordinarily important time for further development of both her oral and written language, before she formally begins to learn to read in first grade.

Up to now I have been giving you teaching strategies

to be used at each stage of a child's development, which roughly parallel specific ages. But now, during these preschool years, each child begins to develop at a more individual pace. And a teaching method that will work with one four-year-old, for example, will not necessarily be right for another child of the same age. So the activities I will talk about next are meant for you to use with your preschool child as she seems able to do them and is interested in them.

Even though your child is now becoming more and more her own person, there are definite personality stages that she will pass through during her preschool years. And it will help you in teaching your child if you have at least a rough idea of what a typical three-year-old, four-year-old, and five-year-old are like.

## THE THREE-YEAR-OLD

The three-year-old has passed through the tumultuous period between babyhood and true childhood known as first adolescence, and is now much more in a state of equilibrium. She is no longer plagued by the anxiety of the transition period. And therefore she no longer needs the protection of her rituals as much. Things no longer need to be done just so. Since she is more flexible, she is much more amenable to being taught new things, including different aspects of reading readiness. In her previous stage she was the world's greatest nonconformist. But now she actually takes pleasure in conforming, in asking her parents for permission, and in pleasing other people.

No longer does everything have to be done her way— or else! She has abdicated as Empress of the Family, the little tyrant who likes to rule over everyone else. She is more able to work patiently at tasks instead of blowing her stack as she did at two and a half. She is able to be more patient about trying to dress herself, or stack a bunch of blocks, or learn a new readiness skill.

Her improved language ability makes her ready for learning many new language skills. She loves new words. Her intellectual horizons are expanding and a whole new world of imagination and fantasy are opening up for her. This is the time, for instance, when she will love to have you read her books of fantasy and imagination.

Three is generally a delightful time for both your child and you. This is a time when your youngster is at peace with herself and her world. She loves life. She loves her parents. And she loves herself. It is an ideal time to teach her anything.


## THE FOUR-YEAR-OLD

Unfortunately, the next year is not quite such an age of harmony. Your child is once again passing through a transition stage, in which she is loosening and breaking up the three-year-old equilibrium, on her way to a newer and more mature phase of equilibrium. Perhaps the best way I can describe the four-year-old is to say that she's very reminiscent of a two-and-a-half-year-old, only more mature and not quite as difficult to get along with.

Four years is a period marked by disequilibrium, insecurity and incoordination. The difficulties you'll notice she has in her relationships with other children will remind you of her two-year-old stage. She is bossy, belligerent, and rambunctious. Many children are as ritualistic at this age as they were at two and a half. They become fixed in their routines, and it may be difficult to get them to tolerate any change in their ways of doing things. This may make teaching your child something new rather difficult.

Dr. Arnold Gesell suggests that the key term for understanding the four-year-old is "out of bounds." She is out of bounds in her motor behavior. She may hit, kick and throw fits of rage. She is out of bounds in her personal relationships. She loves to defy orders and requests.

In spite of all of these potential land mines that may get in the way of teaching your child at this age, she has one important thing going for her. She is fascinated by words, by the sound of words, and by language. Her language behavior takes an immense leap forward. There is also a great spurt of imagination at this age. She loves to make up silly words or to rhyme words. All of this means that it should be much easier to teach reading readiness skills to her now, because her brain is on your side. Her brain is not reluctant to learn words and language; it is eager to learn these things now. She will love to play all sorts of word games with you, and we will talk about these later.

## THE FIVE-YEAR-OLD

Depending on how obnoxious your four-year-old has been, you will probably be grateful for the arrival of the five-year-old stage. Five is usually a delightful age. The out-of-bounds behavior of the four-year-old is gone. Five is usually not in conflict with herself or her environment. She returns to the spirit of cooperation with others that she showed at three, only at a higher level. Emotionally she is well balanced. Intellectually she is full of curiosity and an enthusiasm for learning. She is capable of a great deal intellectually. Presumably she will be in kindergarten this year, so the reading-readiness skills you teach her at home will supplement what she is learning in kindergarten. If your state does not have kindergarten, your home teaching will be even more important for her, in preparing her to learn to read.

You can see that there are enormous psychological differences between a three-, four-, and five-year-old. But with all of these differences, preschool-age children all still share the same task of psychological development. This is to continue to increase their feelings of competence and self-worth. You can help your child by praising her for what she does, rather than criticizing her or putting her down. Try to focus on the positive with your preschooler, even though there may be many times when this seems difficult. Her feeling that she is doing well will help make her eager and competent in trying to learn new things.

At all three ages, preschool children are capable of a great deal of learning. That's why I say they are such golden years for learning reading-readiness skills.

I still remember how my mother helped me greatly with my reading readiness during this stage. I remember her reading a number of books to me before I was old enough for first grade. She used to read to me on the front porch when the weather was nice. During the winter we read in the living room. (Incidentally, my father never read to me, and that is a sad fact of life in all too many American families.)

When I was five, my mother did one of the most important things she had ever done for me. She took me to visit the Enoch Pratt Free Public Library, Branch No. 25 in Baltimore, Maryland, which was about six blocks from where we lived. We went inside, and she showed me the walls lined with bookshelves. She said, "Do you see all those books?"

"Yes."

"Well, when you learn to read, you'll be able to read all of those books. *All of them,*" she repeated. "And here's the best part of it. Do you know how much it will cost you?"

"No, how much?"

"Not a penny."

It's been many, many years since this incident, but I can still hear her saying it: "Not a penny."

"Are you sure, Mother?" (I had been to a number of movies by that time, and I knew it cost money each time.)

"Come here a minute," she said. We went outside and she pointed to the words over the library entrance. "I'm going to read to you what it says up there. It says Enoch Pratt *Free* Public Library, Branch No. 25. See, it's free. It doesn't cost anything to read any of those books."

I remember being absolutely amazed at the incredible expanse of row upon row of books. But mostly I was flabbergasted by the fact that they wouldn't cost me anything to read.

I was really in a sweat to learn how to read so I could start on those books. "C'mon Mom," I urged. "Let's go back inside and look at some of those books."

That's what I hope for your child, that when she becomes five years old she also will "be in a sweat" to learn to read. Her preschool years are a time when her mind is maturing rapidly and she can comprehend increasingly complex oral and written material. There is much you can do to help her developing verbal skills.

*First*, you can continue playing Label the Environment. Only now you will be functioning on a more sophisticated level. What is this? (a brain, in a picture from a book, *What's Inside of Me?*). What is this? (a neon sign).

*Second*, you can continue reading Richard Scarry—such books as *Richard Scarry's Great Big Schoolhouse*, *Richard Scarry's Busy, Busy World*, *Richard Scarry's Busiest People Ever*, *Richard Scarry's Cars and Trucks and Things That Go*, *All Day Long*, *All Year Long*, and *Busy John, Busy People*. Richard Scarry is a tremendous favorite with preschool children, and rightly so.

*Third*, you can continue reading both new and old nursery rhymes to your child, and she will effortlessly continue to learn them by heart.

When she is four, your youngster will particularly like nonsense rhymes, such as "Does A Goat Wear A Coat?" "The Many-Colored Man," "My Silly Self Rhyme," "The Nowhere Zoo," "The Topsy-Turvy Zoo," and "Your Funny Presents" from *I Wish I Had A Computer That Makes Waffles.* And in the final section of this book, you'll find such nonsense poems as "Zero Elephants In My Soup," "A Special Friend of Mine," "If An Ape Can Eat a Grape," "Mr. Ebeneezer Bartholemew Grand," "Mr. McBride," "Is That A Duck?" and "Can An Egg Break A Leg?"

It is easy for adults to miss the point of these rhymes and dismiss them for being "illogical." Actually, they are really poems that train in logical thinking at the preschool level. For your four-year-old will delight in pointing out to you exactly where the poem is wrong.

*Fourth,* you can continue talking to your child, only your conversations will be much more complex and sophisticated than when she was younger. A fun way to stimulate your preschooler's verbal and intellectual skills is to ask her questions like, "What's your opinion about why ice cream melts when you take it out of the refrigerator?" Be prepared for a lot of unscientific answers to these "What's your opinion" questions. But don't feel you have to correct your child at this stage of her development. What you want to do is to encourage her to talk, to talk a lot, and to feel self-confident when she puts her two cents in. There will be many years ahead when she can learn the correct scientific concepts for refrigeration, meteorological phenomena, and the laws of physics and chemistry.

Talk, good talk, is very important for preparing a child to read well. It is no exaggeration to say that children talk their way into reading. They are learning whenever their parents talk to them. But it's even more important for parents to *listen* when their child talks. (Nearly all parents talk to their children, particularly to issue commands, but they often don't *listen.*) The child who learns to read easily and quickly is the child who is self-confident in talking, in expressing her opinions, and in asking questions and giving answers. Her parents listen and respond to her conversation. This child is thoroughly at home in the area of oral language.

*Fifth,* you can do as my mother did many years ago: You can read many books to your child in three years. Parents typically tend to underestimate the innumerable ways in which this teaches her the different reading-readiness skills and thus prepares her for reading. Here are some of the things that happen when you read to her. She sees a role model of an adult who likes to read books. (Children like to imitate role models, particularly parents.) When she is held on your lap, she transfers that pleasant feeling to the feeling of being read to. She learns to pay attention to the words and the phrasing of sentences. She learns how various words are pronounced. She learns how to follow the twists and turns of a story line. Reading a story to her, like talking to her, helps her to learn the structure of the English language. All of these things (and some more technical ones I haven't mentioned) she learns simply by having you read to her! So please—never underestimate how many different things your child will learn when you read her a story. Read her as many as she enjoys, and only stop when she indicates that she doesn't want to hear any more.

Instituting a regular bedtime story ritual at age three will also help to reinforce a love of books and of reading in your youngster. In this ritual, each step follows the preceding one inexorably, as the night follows the day. At a certain time after dinner your child has her bath, which is really a combination of bath and water play. Let her play in the bath with her water toys as long as she likes, and until she tells you she wants to come out. This will relax her thoroughly and prepare her for the next step in the procedure.

Then she goes to her bed, where first her mother reads her a story and then her father does (or the two of you can take turns reading on alternate nights). This reinforces in her the concept that *both* mother and father are concerned with reading. If she begs for another story you may want to give her one more.

Next she has a little bedtime snack, and brushes her teeth. And then it's time to go to sleep. The inclusion of story reading in this bedtime ritual is a powerful reinforcer of both the importance of reading and the love of reading. And, incidentally, this ritual will get your child used to the idea of a regular bedtime.

When you choose a book to read to your child, make sure it is one that interests you. If you like it, then both you and she will probably enjoy reading it. If you make a weekly trip to the library with your child, she will have a weekly reminder of the world of books. Try to keep a rough balance between nonfiction and fiction in the books you choose. Nonfiction gives her valuable information about the world she lives in; fiction helps to stimulate her imagination and creativity.

Don't make the mistake of only getting her books from the library. Buy her some; because if you buy her toys but don't buy her books, she will get the impression that toys are more important than books. So take her to the bookstore regularly and pick out a book for her or help her pick out one for herself. Make a simple bookcase at home for her with slanted display shelves on which her books can be displayed front cover out rather than spine out. Displaying them this way will increase the likelihood that she will pick them up and read them.

Here's another tip. Select several good books by the same author. Then get some information on his personal background from a book called *Something About the Author* (Volumes 1 to 17), which gives facts and pictures about authors of children's books. This series is compiled by

Ann Commire and published by Gale Research Book Tower, Detroit, Michigan. Telling your child about the author as a person usually results in her being much more interested in those books.

Most parents find a guide to children's books very helpful, so I have given you one in Appendix C: a list of both fiction and nonfiction books for youngsters in the preschool stage from three to six.

*Sixth*, you can play Funny Words with your child. I remember first doing this with my son Randy when he was four. One day we were driving over to Grammy's, which was about half an hour away, and we spontaneously invented a new game. It had no name at first, but later I named it Funny Words, and we played it together many times. It was based on nonsense words and went something like this:

Randy: I'm a bleek.
Daddy: I'm a teek.
Randy: I like to eat murfs.
Daddy: I like to eat turfs.
Randy: I smell a squink.
Daddy: I smell a trink.

Randy was absolutely delighted with this game. You can probably begin to play it with your youngster at three. If she doesn't take to it then, she surely will by four, when her interest in words (particularly silly ones) and language makes a massive forward surge. I suggest you start it with nonsense words because they are so easy to come up with, and your child can build up her word confidence by using them.

After she feels thoroughly at home with nonsense words, you can advance one step up to real words that rhyme.

Mother: I like to eat cake.
Janet: I like to watch you bake.
Mother: I like to fly a kite.
Janet: But we can't fly at night.

This game further develops your child's love of words and interest in them. It also helps her to master sounds, and to learn which words sound like which other words. All of these skills are excellent preparation for phonics, word attack skills, and learning to read.

*Seventh,* you can buy your child an inexpensive tape recorder and show her how to use it. The tape recorder is a fantastic learning machine (and a fascinating toy) for a child. But don't simply buy it and give it to her cold. Demonstrate how to use it. Say into it something that will be of interest to her, such as a description of how she looks.

"This is Mommy and I want to tell you about my daughter, Maria. Maria is getting ready to learn to read. She will be a good reader when she learns, because right now she likes to listen to the stories from the books Daddy and I read to her. She likes it when we go to the movies. She likes to go to the ice cream store. She likes to ride her trike. Her favorite breakfast is Total with sliced bananas on top. She also likes pizza and hamburgers and hot dogs. She likes to visit with Grandma and Grandpa because Grandma always bakes her cookies and Grandpa takes her on walks to the park."

Then play this back for your child to hear. Show her how to insert the cartridge and take it out. (Have her practice this and other recording skills immediately after you show her how to do it.) Then show her how to push the button that causes the tape to go forward and play. Show her which buttons to press to have the tape record the sound of her voice. Show her how to rewind the tape.

Then have her make a tape all her own, using the

skills you have just taught her. Ask her if she wants to save the tape to play for Daddy when he gets home.

The usefulness of the tape recorder is limited only by the imagination and creativity of you and your child. For example, you can tape a short chapter from a book and then play it back to her later. Or you can tape nursery rhymes and play them back while she follows them in the book. Or you can play a game of Funny Words on the tape recorder. See what sorts of new and ingenious ways your child can dream up for using the recorder. It is a simply marvelous instrument for developing her oral language.

*Eighth,* you can stimulate your child's language development by showing her how to make her own books.

There are two kinds of books you can teach your child to make. The first is the kind she dictates to you and you print for her. The second and more advanced type is the kind she prints herself. Let's start with the first type.

First, get your materials: 8½-by-11 sheets of paper, felt pens, crayons, stapler, stiff cardboard for covers. Then say something like this to her: "Katie, let's make a book together—your own special book. I'll show you how."

This first book should be about her. Tell her, "This first book will be about you. So let's call it Katie's Book."

"A book is just talk written down. You're going to talk and I'm going to write it down. So what do you want to say about Katie? What does Katie like?"

"Katie likes ice cream."

"Fine. That will be the first page of the book."

You print carefully in caps and lowercase letters, "Katie likes ice cream."

"What else do you want to say about Katie?"

"Katie has a dog named Blacky."

Print that on the next page. Each page will have only the sentence on it. Whatever she says, you print.

"What do you want to say next about Katie?"

"Katie hates to do yard work."

Print that on the next page. Don't try to "improve" on what she tells you or make it "nicer." Write down whatever she says, because it's *her* book, not your book.

And so it goes. Your youngster dictates, and you print it. As long as she's interested in dictating, you write it down. When her interest flags then you know you have come to the end of the book. Decide on an appropriate way to end it and stop. Print with capitals and lowercase letters, just as you would find in a real book. Don't use all capital letters, because you wouldn't find it printed that way in a real book. If your child wants, she can illustrate it with crayon drawings or pictures cut out of magazines.

This book will usually have great meaning for a child, because she has produced it. It is uniquely *her book.*

Future books can be about anything your child wants to talk about: a movie she has seen, her pets, going to the playground, a visit to an amusement park . . . anything!

When the subject matter and the form of the sentences truly come from inside the child, then she has a very powerful motive for wanting to write a book about that subject matter. You know for sure it is something that interests and pleases her. She will usually become highly motivated to continue writing books and thus further develop both her oral and written language skills.

At first your child will dictate the books to you. Later on, when she has learned to print well enough, she can print the book herself, with you telling her how to spell the words. After she has completed her book, take her to a place where it can be Xeroxed. Children are usually fascinated by the Xerox process. With Xeroxing you can produce several copies of the book. These can be sent or given to grandparents or other relatives. If you contact the relative about what you are doing, you can drop a hint for them to send a dollar bill or some other reward back in their letter. This is usually a very powerful incentive for your child to produce more books!

There is probably not a single activity you could do with your child that does more to build her self-confidence in her oral and written language than this method of writing her own books.

*Ninth,* you can teach your child to print, beginning at age three. You need to get an alphabet book from a bookstore that has both uppercase and lowercase letters. Also get a felt-tipped pen, which is much easier for her to use than a pencil or ball-point pen. Buy the kind with water-soluble ink so that you can easily wash "mistakes" off your child's clothes.

Some schoolteachers will tell you that a child should not be taught to print until she is in school, so that the teacher can teach her the "right" way to make the letters. Baloney! There is no "right" way to teach a youngster to print. Teachers often use a chart that supposedly shows how letters should be printed so that the child's printing will flow naturally into cursive writing later. This kind of chart has been an article of faith with schoolteachers for many years. But if you examine the chart closely, as I have, you will see, for example, that the strokes for the letters "v" and "w" are completely wrong. If you teach your child according to such a chart, you will be teaching her to print both "v" and "w" in ways that are quite different from the way she will later cursive-write those two letters.

I think any parent with a modicum of intelligence can teach her child to print, in an unhurried manner, in a one-on-one situation, far better than a hurried teacher who has thirty kids to cope with. Let your child print the letters in any way that is comfortable for her. After all, she's not necessarily going to print them that same way for the rest of her life!

By all means start with the uppercase letters, because they are much easier to learn than lowercase letters. Beginning with the easier ones will help her develop confidence in her ability.

The word that usually holds the most fascination for a child is her own name. So she will usually enjoy learning to print that first. Then you can teach her to print the rest of the letters of the alphabet, but you needn't teach them in order. I think it's best to work from the easier letters to the harder ones. Here is an order of letters that you might use: I,L,X,T,H,F,E,V,O,Q,A,M,N,P,U,C,W,D,Y,Z,K,B,J,R,S,G. But there's nothing sacred about doing it this way. If your child wants to learn some letters that are out of this order, teach her.

It may take your child as long as a year to learn to print these letters. Be patient with her. Simply show her how to make the strokes and let her try it. Praise her for learning each letter, and say nothing about the ones that she may be having trouble with.

The lowercase letters are much harder to learn. So be sure not to teach them until your child has mastered all the capitals. When you get to teaching lowercase, begin by showing your youngster that she already knows some of these letters. They are the ones that are exactly the same as the capitals, only smaller: o,c,i,v,w,s,u,x, and z (except that the lower case "i" has a dot over it, and the uppercase one doesn't).

There are some other educational aids that will help your child learn. You can buy magnetic letters at a toy store and stick them on the refrigerator door. Fisher-Price has good sets of both capitals and lowercase. You can leave little words on the refrigerator for your child. Or you can leave such messages as "Kim ice cream," and then tell her what the words mean and give her some ice cream as a reward. Such messages powerfully increase your child's motivation to learn to read!

You can also make sandpaper letters yourself. Simply draw letters onto cardboard, cut them out, and glue sandpaper to the backs. Then your child can trace the shape of the letter with her fingers. The advantage of using sandpaper letters is that she is using a sense modality (touch) to learn the letters. You can play a game with her in which you hand her the letter from behind and she has to trace the shape with her fingers and figure it out. You can have some kind of special treat after playing the game. (This does not mean you will have to keep rewarding her forever for playing these kinds of games. As she learns the letters and then words, she will enjoy playing them just for the fun of learning.)

Here are some other materials you can use in getting your child interested in printing. Go to an Instant Press shop and have your child's own stationery printed, with her name in big letters at the top. You can also get some 4 × 6 cards printed with her name, which she can print on and mail.

Big rubber stamps of the alphabet letters will be much loved by your child. Get both caps and lowercase letters. These may be hard to find but they are worth the trouble. Educational supply stores usually have them. Using a stamp pad, your child can spell out words and sentences. The use of rubber stamps helps to teach the recognition of the alphabet through physical involvement.

One good way to motivate your child for printing is to get her involved in making lists of different things. A list of what she wants you to buy at the store. A list of Christmas or birthday presents that she wants. A list of clothes she wants you to buy for her. A list of her favorite things to eat.

Practice in printing reinforces many of the skills that your child will need in order to get ready to learn to read. Printing and reading go hand in hand and reinforce each other.

If you start at age three, even if your child goes very slowly she will know how to print all the uppercase and lowercase letters by the time she enters kindergarten. She will thereby have an enormous head start in school.

Once your child has mastered her letters, you can play the "Give Your Child a Word" game. You begin by asking her to tell you a word, any word at all. She tells you a word (perhaps "monster") and you tell her how to print it, letter by letter, on a 3 × 5 card. She can carry it around with her all day. That is her word for the day. Don't worry if some of the words sound terrible to you (like "bloody" or "murder"). They are *her* words and she will be interested in them because she has chosen them herself.

Well, there you have it, the step-by-step program of how your child can learn to read with her brain for five years before she is formally taught to read in school. If you follow all these suggestions, you are going to do fantastic things to give her a head start in reading.

I hope you have already begun talking to your baby and singing to her. If you have, you realize what fun it's going to be for *you*, to enrich your child's storehouse of verbal information.

I have spent most of this book telling you what this planned program of reading readiness will do for your child. I want to close by telling you what it will do for *you*.

Many parents do not really know what to do with preschool children. They spend much of their time riding herd on them to keep them out of mischief. You will not be like that. You will spend a lot of time playing enjoyably with your child. But the enjoyable play will also be educational. It will be teaching her reading-readiness skills, so that learning to read in first grade will be easy and pleasurable for her. Every parent wants to make her child's entry into school as smooth as possible. Every parent wants to put the first five years when his child is his alone to the best possible use. With the help of this book, you will know exactly how to do that.

And when you play the educational games of this reading-readiness program, you will be fascinated to see your child progress from one developmental level of language skills to the next. Not only will the whole teaching process be a joy, but you will find it has helped reinforce your close and loving relationship with your child through the things you have shared. It will help you realize the truth of the poet John Masefield's saying, "The days that make us happy make us wise."

# III I Wish I Had a Computer That Makes Ice Cream Cones

Here is a collection of modern nursery rhymes, *I Wish I Had a Computer That Makes Ice Cream Cones*, which you can read to your child as an important part of his oral language development. You can use these rhymes from the time he is one and a half until he is about six. Even after he is able to recite them himself, he will still enjoy hearing them from you.

Simply reading these delightful rhymes to him in his very early, formative years will foster a number of reading-readiness skills.

This is what he will begin to learn:

1. to listen carefully and pay attention
2. to discriminate among words that sound alike, but are different
3. to be curious about words
4. to speak words and sentences clearly and correctly, as he repeats the rhymes after you recite them
5. to have a developing oral vocabulary
6. to love language and the cadence of words

7. to be curious about the varied information to be found in the world, including the world of books

8. to have a good imagination

9. to be able to think, particularly as he figures out the "nonsense" rhymes

10. to express himself and have self-confidence in trying new things, such as reciting parts of the rhymes, and finally, the whole rhymes

11. to be eager to learn to read the rhymes himself, as he gets to be five years old

When you first start reading the rhymes to your child, sit him on your lap so that he associates reading with a cozy seat on Mother or Daddy's lap. The illustrations are striking and children love them, so make optimum use of them as you read. Point out things in the pictures or have him point them out. Say things like, "See if you can find the giraffe." or "Where did the snowman go?"

Don't try to get him to memorize the verses. Simply read them over and over, and he will, without any effort, learn them by heart. When he is old enough to have done this, try leaving out a word and see if he can fill it in. If he can't, simply read the word yourself and go on.

If your child indicates in any way that he is tired of having you read, then stop. He knows when he has had enough, so be alert to his clues.

Perhaps I should say a word about the title. My first book of modern nursery rhymes was called *I Wish I Had a Computer That Makes Waffles.* It turned out to be probably the most intriguing title of any book I have written. It grew out of a line in one of the rhymes. It was such a fun title that I decided to make this one similar to the first one. So, having created the title, I wrote a nursery rhyme to go with it. And here it is!

# My Computer Makes Ice Cream Cones

My dog's computer
Makes juicy bones,
But my computer
Makes ice cream cones.

Vanilla, strawberry,
Lemon, or lime,
My computer makes ice cream
All the time!

# I Wish I Had a Robot

I wish I had a robot;
I'd name him Mister Click.
He'd have to take my medicine
When I am cross and sick.

I wish I had a robot
Who could light up his big nose;
He'd go in my dark closet
And hang up all my clothes.

I wish I had a robot
Made just for girls and boys;
He would come and play with me,
Then pick up all my toys.

I wish I had a robot
Looking just like me.
He could take my place
When I wanted to be free.

# Zero Elephants in My Soup

There are zero elephants in my soup;
Zero airplanes playing loop the loop.
There are zero railroads in the sea;
And zero submarines in my tree.
There are zero zebras in the family room;
Zero helicopters on mother's broom.
There are zero fish up in the sky;
Zero whales in trucks driving by.
There are zero giraffes watching TV;
And zero lions playing chess with me.

## The Rain, the Wind, and the Snow

Raindrops pitter-patter;
Wind whispers through the trees.
But snow comes down without a sound
And piles up to my knees.

## The Wonder of the Grass

The grass is very different
From a carpet or a street.
It feels so soft and wiggly
Under my bare feet.

## A Special Friend of Mine

William is a friend of mine;
We rassle round and round.
I pounce on him, I bounce on him;
He throws me to the ground.

William lets me ride his back;
I pull him in my wagon.
But Mom won't let him in the house
'Cause William is a dragon!

## The Sky Is All Around

The rabbits are thumping
And the sky is all around.
The dump trucks are dumping
And the sky is all around.
The horses are dashing
And the sky is all around.
The fountains are splashing
And the sky is all around.
The babies are crying
And the sky is all around.
The airplanes are flying
And the sky is all around.
The donkeys are braying
And the sky is all around.
The children are playing
And the sky is all around.

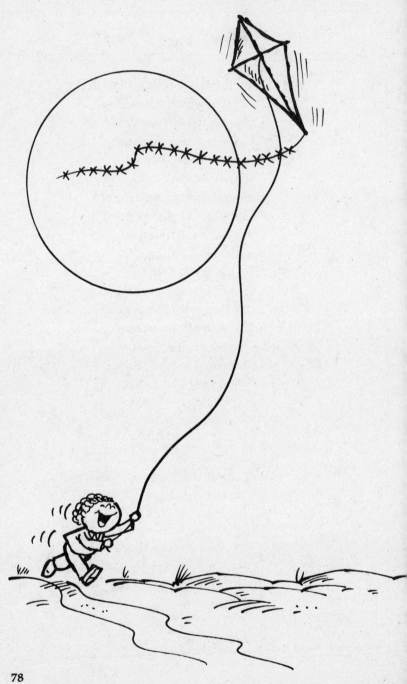

# Things We Can Do

A shoe we can tie,
A kite we can fly.
A song we can sing,
A bell we can ring.

A balloon we can blow,
A boat we can row.
A bed we can make,
A bath we can take.

A cat we can feed,
A book we can read.
A prayer we can say,
A piano we can play.

A seed we can sow,
A plant we can grow.
A walk we can take,
A lawn we can rake.

A tale we can tell,
A word we can spell.
A pie we can bake,
A rug we can shake.

# The Big Red Bus

The mouse picked up a house
And put it on his back.
The kitten picked up a mitten
And put it on his back.
The fish picked up a dish
And put it on his back.
The dog picked up a log
And put it on his back.
The sheep picked up a jeep
And put it on his back.
The duck picked up a truck
And put it on his back.
The goose picked up a moose
And put it on his back.
And they all got on the bus,
The big red bus.
Yes they all rode the bus,
The big red bus.
The mouse and the house,
The kitten and the mitten,
The fish and the dish,
The dog and the log,
The sheep and the jeep,
The duck and the truck,
The goose and the moose.
They were all crowded in,
Like sardines in a tin.
Without a bit of fuss,
On the big red bus!

# Vacation

On vacation we drive
To a big green park
And toast our hot dogs
In the dark.

I like to camp out
In a tent made for three.
With a place for my mom
And my dad and me.

I like the birds,
The squirrel and bees.
I like to run
And climb the trees.

And when it's time
To pack our gear,
I know we'll be back
Again next year!

# If an Ape Can Eat a Grape

If an ape
Can eat a grape,
Can a goose
Drink orange juice?
If a seal
Can eat a meal,
Can a flea
Drink milk and tea?
If a pig
Can eat a fig,
Can a spider
Drink apple cider?

## My Trike

I'm too small for a bike
So I ride my trike.
I speed down the walk
So fast I can't talk.
I ride low to the ground
As I turn it around.
There's nothing so fine
As this trike of mine!

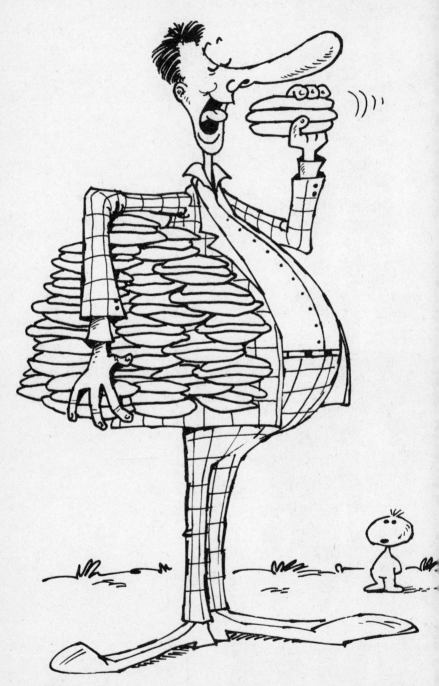

## Mr. Ebeneezer Bartholemew Grand

Mr. Ebeneezer Bartholemew Grand
Is the tallest man in the land.
His nose is as big as an ice cream store,
You can hear him for miles when he starts to snore.
His feet are as wide as a big Mexican hat,
And if he steps on a car he squashes it flat!
His stomach's as big as a ferris wheel,
And he eats a hundred hot dogs at every meal!

# Fighting and Making Up

There once was a sister and brother
Who used to get mad at each other.
They'd stamp and they'd glare,
Even sometimes pull hair.
"Enough of that—stop it!" said Mother.
Then one would break out in a smile,
And they would make up in a while.
They'd find something to play
For the rest of the day
That was better than fighting each other!

# Why

Why does a kitty cat climb a tree?
Why does a puppy scratch for a flea?
Why does a rooster stretch his neck?
Why do birds eat seeds by the peck?
Why does a cow chew her cud?
Why does a pig wallow in mud?
Why does a horse walk clippity-clop?
Why does a bunny go hippity-hop?
Why does a cow always say "Moo"?
Why does a ghost always say "Boo"?
Why do the flowers bloom in the spring?
Why does the phone go ting-a-ling?

# If I Were a Cat

If I were a kitty cat
Now wouldn't that be grand?
I'd purr and rub against you,
I'd jump up and lick your hand.

I could tease the dog next door
Because he chases me.
I'd arch my back and hiss at him,
Then run right up a tree.

I'd roll and romp in summertime,
Dirt can be such fun.
I'd make believe I'm hiding,
Then up I'd jump and run.

Even winter's snow is great,
Tumbling down on me.
I'd leap around and try to hide,
Then peek out just to see.

Yes I'd like to be a cat,
So happy and so free.
Even though it's just pretend,
That's what I'd like to be!

# Wonderful, Wonderful Mud

Mother says
That mud's a mess.
But mud to me
Is happiness!

# My Bath

I think a bath is lots of fun
Surrounded by my toys.
I sail my boat through bubbles high;
It makes a splendid noise.

But later on when Daddy showers
He doesn't think it's fun
To find the bathtub filled with toys;
So I pick up every one.

# The Room in the Mirror

I have another playroom
In the mirror on my door.
The ceiling is the same as mine,
So are the walls and floor.
But everything is rearranged—
Backwards, is what I mean,
And to see it clearly
The mirror must be clean.
When my room needs straightening up,
I work until it's done.
I look, and there, to my surprise,
I've cleaned the other one!

# Tiny and Enormous

Tiny is the lightning bug,
Blinking in the night.
Small is the furry mouse,
Scampering out of sight.
Large is the gentle cow,
Munching in her stall.
Enormous is the elephant,
Biggest of them all!

# Mr. McBride

Mr. McBride is a funny old man;
He drinks his milk from a frying pan.
He combs his hair with a butter knife;
It's the craziest thing you've seen in your life!
He fills his pockets with vanilla ice cream;
When they start to drip he lets out a scream!
He washes his clothes in lemonade,
And always dries them in the shade.
People laugh at Mr. McBride;
They don't know he's smiling inside.

# Is That a Duck?

Is that a bear
Combing his hair?
Is that a snake
Skating on the lake?
Is that a mouse
Building a house?
Is that a pig squealing
Up on the ceiling?
Is that a duck
Driving my truck?

## My Body

My eyes are for winking,
My mind is for thinking,
My ears are for hearing,
My hair is for shearing.
My arms are for squeezing,
My nose is for sneezing,
My legs are for walking,
My mouth is for talking.
My toes are for wiggling,
My legs are for jiggling,
My hands are for catching,
My back is for scratching.
I'm wrapped up in my skin,
Just like in a rug,
These parts are my body,
All ready to hug!

# The Magic of Sand

Sand is glorious magical stuff;
I never can seem to get enough.
I grab a fistful of nice warm sand,
But somehow it slips right through my hand.
I pack it with water in a cup
And then I'm able to firm it up.
Now I can press it tightly down
And build myself a little town.
A little town with houses and forts;
To make it with water I have to use quarts!

# Cloud Animals

Fluffy, friendly dragons
Float across the sky.
Shapes of whales and dinosaurs
That swim and soar and fly.

I like to watch the changing clouds;
Their shapes are fun to see.
And as they frolic on fields of blue,
Do they look down at me?

# Tying My Shoe

Tying my shoe
Isn't easy to do
With hands as small as mine.
Twisting the laces
In all the right places
Is a puzzle that really takes time.
First my foot goes in the shoe;
I pull the strings back tight.
But is it right one over left
Or left one over right?
Some day I will do it,
If I can stick to it,
A very neat knot and a bow.
Please be patient with me
For I'm just learning, you see,
So I'll take it a little bit slow.

## Before I Go to Sleep

I like to sit on Daddy's lap;
At night it's warm and cozy.
I listen to him read to me
Till I get kind of dozy.
Then he carries me to bed
And tucks me in real tight.
I feel him kiss my cheek
And hear him say "Good Night."

## I Lost My Snowman

I made a snowman
Round and fat;
I dressed him in style
With a coat and a hat.

The sun smiled down
To see him there.
Then he disappeared!
I don't know where.

He left his clothes
All sopping wet.
And I haven't found
My snowman yet!

# The Wishing Boy

I wish I could fly an airplane
Up in the wide blue sky.
I wish I could climb a tall, tall tree
And watch the cars go by.
I wish I was a carpenter
And could build a house for you.
I wish I could drive a great big bus
And take children to the zoo.
I wish I could go on a fishing boat
And catch an enormous fish.
It's fun to be a little boy,
And wish and wish and wish!

## An Ecology Song

Pick up the litter
On the ground,
Until there's no more
To be found!
We'll make this town
So nice and clean
That you can tell
The grass is green.

## If I Were an Animal

I'd like to be an elephant
So big and fat and gray;
With my long and curly trunk
I'd feed myself all day!

Wouldn't it be fun to have
A neck like a giraffe?
Every time I heard a joke
I'd have eleven feet of laugh!

I'd like to be a centipede;
A hundred legs are nifty.
If I got tired in half my legs
I'd use the other fifty!

If I were a snail I'd go ever so slow;
I'd never overdo.
Just to get myself to school
Might take a month or two!

If I were a lion, to roar and roar
Would be one of my greatest joys.
But I'd put earplugs in my ears
To keep out all the noise!

To be a camel would be odd;
My back would have two humps.
People who saw me would surely think
My backbone had the mumps!

Well that's how the game is played;
Don't you think it's fun?
Just think of any animal
And make believe you're one.

# Feet

Feet are big and feet are small.
Feet hold up people short and tall.
To climb the stairs or cross the street,
Would be impossible without feet.
Just think how funny marching bands
Would look, parading on their hands!

# Can an Egg Break a Leg?

If weasels
Catch measles,
Can a fox
Get chicken pox?
If a goat
Has a sore throat,
Can an egg
Break a leg?
If a yak
Sprains his back,
Can a gnu
Catch the flu?

# Wet and Wetter

Raindrops fall and I can't play
Because I would get wet.
So why do I have to take a bath
And get much wetter yet?

# The Puddle Mirror

Look down in a puddle,
Because if you do,
You'll see someone in it
Looking right back at you!

# Gregory, Gregory!

Gregory, Gregory, I declare!
Can that be oatmeal in your hair?
Gregory, Gregory, do you suppose
That's strawberry jam on your nose?
Gregory, Gregory, what have we here?
Chocolate pudding in your ear?
Gregory, Gregory, what did you do?
Gregory, Gregory, I love you!

## Sometimes

Sometimes I'd like to be a turtle, with a big thick
    shell;
When I go on a trip I wear my hotel?
Sometimes I'd like to be a lion, brave and strong;
King of the jungle, that's where I belong.
Sometimes I'd like to be a bird in the sky,
Where the air is so clear and the clouds tumble by.
But sometimes I think I'd rather just be
My own special self, nobody but me!

# My Favorite Toys

My pounding bench goes bang, bang, bang!
I love to hear the noise.
But Mommy's brand new pots and pans
Are still my favorite toys.

# APPENDIX A
# MUSIC OF MANY CULTURES
# FOR INFANTS

Only recently has research shown us how sensitive babies are to their environment, through the avenues of sight, hearing, touch, and smell. I believe it is a very good thing for parents to play music of many cultures to young babies. Although your baby may make no outward response, the music is being filed away in the computer brain of that lovely little head, for use later on. And your baby is learning to distinguish the quite different sounds and melodies coming from a variety of cultures. By learning to discriminate among sounds, she is acquiring an important skill that she will need in learning how to read.

## FOLK

1. *Carlos Chavez—The Four Suns and Selections from "Piramide"* (Mexico) (Columbia)
2. *Olatunji! Drums of Passion* (Columbia)
3. *International Folk Dance Mixer* (includes music from Africa, Denmark, Scotland, Italy, Israel, Russia, etc.) (Gateway)

4. *Hora-Songs and Dances of Israel,* Geula Gill (Electra)
5. *Lilacs Out of the Dead Land* (Greek), Manos Hadjidakis (Phillips)
6. *Jazayer* (Egypt) (Jazayer Co.)
7. *Musical Instruments of Africa,* Vol. I, strings (Kaleidophone)
8. *Fiesta Mexicana,* Javier de Leon (Monitor)
9. *El Mejor Mariachi Del Mundo,* Vol. I, Mariachi Tecatitlan (Mexico)
10. *Flower Drum and Other Chinese Folk Songs* (Monitor)
11. *Jatari!!* (South America) (Monitor)
12. *Russian Folk Dances of the Moiseyev Dance Company* (Monitor)
13. *Songs and Dances of Vietnam* (Monitor)
14. *Africa Drum, Chant and Instruental Music* (Nonesuch)
15. *Flower Dance* (Japanese, includes koto, shamisen, drums, etc.) (Nonesuch)
16. *El Autentico Tamborazo Zacatecano* (Mexico) (Orefon)
17. *Bailes Folkloricos de Mexico* (Peerless)
18. *Juegos Infantiles de Mexico,* Vol. I (RCA)
19. *Israeli Folk Dances,* Martha Schlamme and Mort Freeman (Israel)
20. *The Sound of the Sun* (Trionidad), The Westland Steel Band (Nonesuch)

## CLASSICAL

1. *Piano music of Erik Satie*—Vol. 3—Includes "The Puppets Are Dancing," "Picturesque Childishnesses," etc. (Angel)
2. Bowmar Orchestral Library: This series of records takes a central theme in orchestral music and presents different composers' pieces around that central theme. Listed below are five excellent recordings, and many more are available (Bowmar).

a) *Twentieth Century America*—Copeland (*El Salón México*); Bernstein (Excerpts, Symphonic Dances from *West Side Story*); Gershwin (*An American in Paris*), etc.

b) *Masters of Music*—Mahler (Symphony #1); Brahms (Hungarian Dance #6); Wagner ("The Ride of the Valkyries"); etc.

c) *Fantasy in Music*—Prokofiev (*Cinderella Suite*); Tschaikovsky (*Sleeping Beauty*); etc.

d) *Animals and Circus*—Saint-Saëns (*Carnival of the Animals*); Stravinsky ("Circus Polka"); etc.

e) *Overtures*—Rossini (Overture to *William Tell*); Mozart (Overture to *The Marriage of Figaro*); etc.

3. *The Small Listener*—Includes many short compositions by Haydn, Schubert, Bartok, Mozart, etc. (Bowmar)

4. *Bernstein Conducts Copeland*—Includes *El Salón México*, *Appalachian Spring*, etc. (Columbia)

5. *Wind Song*—Includes "Wind Song" by Paul Chihara, Excerpts from "The Children's Corner Suite" by Debussy, etc. (Everest)

## RESTING TIME MUSIC—FOR REST AND RELAXATION

1. *Nocturne*—Leonard Bernstein and the New York Philharmonic play Nocturne from *Carmen*, "Dawn" from *Peer Gynt*, "Greensleeves," etc. (Columbia)

2. *Spectrum Suite*—Steve Halpern (Halpern Sounds Records)

3. *Four Centuries of Music for the Harp*—Includes music by Bach, Handel, Palero, etc. (Nonesuch)

4. *Clair De Lune*—Eugene Ormandy and the Philadelphia Orchestra—Includes "The Swan," Three Nocturnes, etc. (Columbia)

5. *Serenade For Strings*—Eugene Ormandy and the Philadelphia Orchestra play Tschaikovsky ("Serenade for Strings"), Borodin ("Nocturne for Strings"), etc. (Columbia)

## JAZZ

1. *Viva Bossa Nova*, Laurindo Almeida (Capitol)
2. *The Best of Louis Armstrong* (MCA)
3. *The Best of John Coltrane* (Impulse)
4. *Black Satin*, The George Shearing Quintet (Capitol)
5. *Bola Sete and Friends*, Vince Guarardi (Fantasy)
6. *The Best of Chico Hamilton* (Impulse)
7. *Inside*—Paul Horn plays inside the Taj Mahal (Epic)
8. *Jamalca*, Ahmad Jamal (20th Century)
9. *Bella Via*, Chuck Mangione (A and M)
10. *The Chuck Mangione Quartet.* (Mercury)
11. *The Best of Wes Montgomery*—Includes "The Shadow Of Your Smile," etc. (Verve)
12. *The Red Back Book*—music of Scott Joplin played by the New England Conservatory Ragtime Ensemble. Includes "Maple Leaf Rag," "The Entertainer," etc. (Angel)

# APPENDIX B
# BOOKS FOR FIRST
# ADOLESCENCE

1. *No Ducks in Our Bathtub*, Martha Alexander (Dial, also paperback)
2. *A Friend Is Someone Who Likes You*, Joan Walsh Anglund (Harcourt Brace)
3. *What Does the Rooster Say, Yoshio?*, Edith Battles (Albert Whitman)
4. *What I hear*, June Behrens (A. W. Children's)
5. *Bow Wow! A First Book of Sounds*, Melanie Bellah (Golden Press)
6. *Johnny Crow's Garden*, Leslie Brooke (Watts, also paperback)
7. *A Child's Goodnight Book*, Margaret Wise Brown (A. W. Children's)
8. *The City Noisy Book*, Margaret Wise Brown (Harper & Row)
9. *The Country Noisy Book*, Margaret Wise Brown (Harper & Row)
10. *Goodnight Moon*, Margaret Wise Brown (Harper & Row, also paperback)
11. *The Indoor Noisy Book*, Margaret Wise Brown (Harper & Row)

12. *The Noisy Book*, Margaret Wise Brown (Harper & Row)
13. *The Quiet Noisy Book*, Margaret Wise Brown (Harper & Row)
14. *The Runaway Bunny*, Margaret Wise Brown (Harper & Row, also paperback)
15. *The Seashore Noisy Book*, Margaret Wise Brown (Harper & Row)
16. *The Summer Noisy Book*, Margaret Wise Brown (Harper & Row)
17. *The Winter Noisy Book*, Margaret Wise Brown (Harper & Row, also paperback)
18. *Where Have You Been?* Margaret Wise Brown (Hastings)
19. *It Does Not Say Meow*, Beatrice DeRegniers (Seabury)
20. *Just Me*, Marie Ets (Viking and also Penguin paperback)
21. *Play with Me*, Marie Ets (Viking and Golden Press paperback)
22. *The Story about Ping*, Marjorie Flack (Viking and also Penguin paperback)
23. *Look Around and Listen*, Jay Friedman (Grosset & Dunlap, paperback)
24. *Millions of Cats*, Wanda Gag (Coward, McCann, also paperback)
25. *Everybody Has a House and Everybody Eats*, Mary McBurney Green (A. W. Children's)
26. *Animal Daddies and My Daddy*, Barbara Hazen (Golden Press)
27. *Bedtime for Frances*, Russell Hoban (Harper & Row, also paperback)
28. *A Birthday for Frances*, Russell Hoban (Harper & Row, also paperback)
29. *Bread and Jam for Frances*, Russell Hoban (Harper & Row, also Scholastic paperback)
30. *Big Red Bus*, Ethel Kessler (Doubleday)

31. *The Day Daddy Stayed Home*, Ethel and Leonard Kessler (Doubleday, also paperback)
32. *Goodnight ABC*, Robert Kraus (Dutton)
33. *The Carrot Seed*, Ruth Kraus (Harper & Row and Scholastic Book Service paperback)
34. *Swimmy*, Leo Lionni (Pantheon, also paperback)
35. *Make Way for Ducklings*, Robert McCloskey (Viking and also Penguin paperback)
36. *Little Bear*, Else Minarik (Harper & Row, also paperback)
37. *Bedtime*, Beni Montresor (Harper & Row)
38. *I Hear: Sounds in a Child's World*, Lucille Ogle and Tina Thoburn (American Heritage Press)
39. *The Tale of Peter Rabbit*, Beatrix Potter (Warne)
40. *Daddies, What They Do All Day*, Helen Puner (Lothrop)
41. *Goodnight Andrew, Goodnight Craig*, Marjorie Sharmatt (Harper & Row)
42. *Daddy Book*, R. Steward and D. Madden (McGraw-Hill)
43. *Days With Daddy*, Pauline Watson (Prentice-Hall)
44. *Harry the Dirty Dog*, Gene Zion (Harper & Row, also paperback)
45. *Summer Night*, Charlotte Zolotow (Harper & Row)

# APPENDIX C
# A PARENT'S GUIDE TO BOOKS
# FOR CHILDREN FROM
# THREE TO SIX

The ages from three to six are golden years for enriching your child's oral and written language devleopment. One of the best ways of doing this is to read to him. Many parents do not know what good books are available for preschoolers, so I have provided this list. Please do not feel you should read *all* the books on the list. I have given you such an immense list so that you can pick and choose as you would at a cafeteria. Obviously nobody chooses *all* the food available at a cafeteria, and you will not have time to choose all this educational food for your child.

Incidentally, many parents think that if their library does not have a book they are out of luck. Not so. Usually your library can get the book for you on interlibrary loan.

It's important to read your child a good mix of nonfiction and fiction. Nonfiction teaches your child concepts that will help him understand his world. Fiction enlarges his imagination and stimulates his creative thinking.

## "BEFORE AND AFTER" BEGINNING
## TO READ BOOKS.

I call these "before and after" books for a simple reason. You can read them to your child between three and six, before he has learned to read. Then, later, as he is learning to read, he can read them himself. He will regard these books as old, familiar friends, rather than as frightening strangers, with unfamiliar words. Thus his self-confidence will increase as he learns to read them.

All these books are written specifically for children who are beginning to read. I have listed each of these eighteen beginning-to-read series by publisher, in order to make it easy for you to become familiar with them.

A. **Children's Press: Stepping into Science series**
 1. *Ecology and Pollution: Air*, Martin Gutnick
 2. *Ecology and Pollution: Land*, Martin Gutnick
 3. *Ecology and Pollution: Water*, Martin Gutnick
 4. *Sounds All About*, Illa Podendorf
 5. *Easy or Hard? That's a Good Question*, Tobi Tobias
 6. *Liquid or Solid? That's a Good Question*, Tobi Tobias
 7. *Quiet or Noisy? That's a Good Question*, Tobi Tobias

B. **Children's Press: The True Book series**
 1. *The True Book of Metric Measurement*, June Behrens
 2. *The True Book of Dinosaurs*, Mary Lou Clark
 3. *The True Book of the Moonwalk Adventure*, Margaret Friskey
 4. *The True Book of the Mars Landing*, Leila Gemme

C. **Coward, McCann: Science Is What and Why Series**
 1. *Rocks All Around*, Margaret Bartlett
 2. *Fitting In: Animals in Their Habitats*, Gilda and Melvin Berger
 3. *Atoms*, Melvin Berger
 4. *Computers*, Melvin Berger
 5. *Stars*, Melvin Berger
 6. *Time After Time*, Melvin Berger
 7. *Sand*, Sally Cartwright
 8. *Sunlight*, Sally Cartwright
 9. *Water Is Wet*, Sally Cartwright
 10. *What's in a Map?* Sally Cartwright

11. *Who Will Drown the Sound?* Carleen Hutchins
12. *Friction,* Howard Liss
13. *Heat,* Howard Liss
14. *Levers,* Lisa Miller
15. *Sound,* Lisa Miller
16. *Who Will Wash the River?* Wallace Orlowsky
17. *Your Brain Power,* Gretchen and Thomas Perera
18. *Who Will Clean the Air?* Thomas R. Perera
19. *Motion,* Seymour Simon
20. *Look! How Your Eyes See,* Marcel Sislowitz
21. *Sunpower,* Norman Smith

D. **Thomas Y. Crowell: Let's Read and Find Out science books**
This series is excellent. It is difficult to praise it too highly. The scientific information is accurate and up-to-date. The format of the books is splendid, and the illustrations are eye-catching.

1. *My Five Senses,* Aliki (also paperback)
2. *My Hands,* Aliki
3. *Hot as an Icecube,* Philip Balestrino
4. *Animals in Winter,* Henrietta Bancroft and Richard Van Gelder
5. *Where the Brook Begins,* Margaret Bartlett
6. *Energy from the Sun,* Melvin Berger
7. *Air Is All Around You,* Franklyn Branley
8. *The Beginning of the Earth,* Franklyn Branley
9. *The Moon Seems to Change,* Franklyn Branley
10. *North, South, East and West,* Franklyn Branley
11. *Rain and Hail,* Franklyn Branley
12. *Rockets and Satellites,* Franklyn Branley
13. *Snow Is Falling,* Franklyn Branley
14. *The Sun: Our Nearest Star,* Franklyn Branley
15. *What Makes Day and Night?* Franklyn Branley (also paperback)
16. *What the Moon Is Like,* Franklyn Branley (also paperback)

17. *What Makes a Shadow?* Clyde Bulla
18. *Birds Eat and Eat and Eat,* Roma Gans (also paperback)
19. *Caves,* Roma Gans
20. *It's Nesting Time,* Roma Gans (also paperback)
21. *Bees and Beelines,* Judy Hawes (also paperback)
22. *Ladybug, Ladybug,* Judy Hawes (also paperback)
23. *Watch Honeybees with Me,* Judy Hawes
24. *How a Seed Grows,* Helene Jordan (also paperback)
25. *Seeds by Wind and Water,* Helene Jordan
26. *A Map Is a Picture,* Barbara Rinkoff
27. *A Baby Starts to Grow,* Paul Showers (also paperback)
28. *Before You Were a Baby,* Paul Showers and Kay Showers
29. *Find Out by Touching,* Paul Showers
30. *Follow Your Nose,* Paul Showers (also paperback)
31. *Hear Your Heart,* Paul Showers (also paperback)
32. *How You Talk,* Paul Showers (also paperback)
33. *Look at Your Eyes,* Paul Showers (also paperback)
34. *Me and My Family Tree,* Paul Showers
35. *The Listening Walk,* Paul Showers
36. *Where Does the Garbage Go?* Paul Showers
37. *Your Skin and Mine,* Paul Showers (also paperback)
38. *Camels: Ships of the Desert,* John F. Waters
39. *Hungry Sharks,* John F. Waters

E. **Follett: Beginning to Read series**
1. *The Strange Hotel: Five Ghost Stories,* Marcy Carafoli (also paperback)
2. *Beginning to Read Riddles and Jokes,* Alice Gilbreath (also paperback)
3. *Have You Seen My Brother?* Elizabeth Guilfoile
4. *Nobody Listens to Andrew,* Elizabeth Guilfoile (also paperback)
5. *The Birthday Cake,* Margaret Hillert (also paperback)

6. *Come Play with Me,* Margaret Hillert (also paperback)
7. *The Funny Baby,* Margaret Hillert (also paperback)
8. *Happy Birthday, Dear Dragon,* Margaret Hillert (also paperback)
9. *Little Puff,* Margaret Hillert
10. *Little Runaway,* Margaret Hillert (also paperback)
11. *The Magic Beans,* Margaret Hillert (also paperback)
12. *George Washington,* Clara Judson (also paperback)
13. *An Elephant in My Bed,* Suzanne Klein (also paperback)
14. *You Are What You Are,* Valjean McLenighan (also paperback)
15. *The Curious Cow,* Esther Meeks (only Scholastic paperback)
16. *A Frog Sandwich: Riddles and Jokes,* Marci Ridlon
17. *Kittens and More Kittens,* Marci Ridlon (also paperback)
18. *The First Thanksgiving,* Lou Rogers
19. *Banji's Magic Wheel,* Letta Schatz
20. *Crocodiles Have Big Teeth All Day,* Mary Smith
21. *The Boy Who Wouldn't Say His Name,* Elizabeth Vreeken (also paperback)
22. *One Day Everything Went Wrong,* Elizabeth Vreeken (also paperback)
23. *The Ice Cream Cone,* Mildred Willard
24. *The No-Bark Dog,* Stanford Williamson

F. **Follett: Beginning Science series**
   1. *Light,* Isaac Asimov
   2. *The Moon,* Isaac Asimov
   3. *The Solar System,* Isaac Asimov
   4. *Earth Through the Ages,* Philip Carona
   5. *Water,* Philip Carona
   6. *Your Wonderful Body,* Robert Follett
   7. *Your Wonderful Brain,* Mary J. Keeney
   8. *Weather,* Julian May

9. *Rocks and Minerals,* Lou Page
10. *Electricity,* Edward Victor
11. *Friction,* Edward Victor
12. *Fishes,* Loren Woods

G. **Harper & Row: Early I Can Read Books**
1. *And I Mean It,* Crosby Bonsall
2. *The Day I Had to Play with My Sister,* Crosby Bonsall
3. *Hattie Rabbit,* Dick Gackenbach
4. *Barkley,* Syd Hoff
5. *The Horse in Harry's Room,* Syd Hoff
6. *Who Will Be My Friend?* Syd Hoff
7. *Come and Have Fun,* Edith Hurd
8. *Cat and Dog,* Else Minarik
9. *Dinosaur Time,* Peggy Parrish

H. **Harper & Row: I Can Read Books**
1. *Little Runner of the Longhouse,* Betty Baker
2. *Oscar Otter,* Nathaniel Benchley
3. *Who's a Pest?* Crosby Bonsall
4. *Animal Doctors: What Do They Do?* Carla Greene
5. *Cowboys: What Do They do?* Carla Greene
6. *Doctors and Nurses: What Do They Do?* Carla Greene
7. *Policemen and Firemen: What Do They Do?* Carla Green
8. *Truck Drivers: What Do They Do?* Carla Greene
9. *The Happy Birthday Present,* John Heilbroner
10. *Arthur's Pen Pal,* Lillian Hoban
11. *Arthur's Prize Reader,* Lillian Hoban
12. *Tom and the Two Handles,* Russell Hoban
13. *Danny and the Dinosaur,* Syd Hoff
14. *Grizzwold,* Syd Hoff
15. *Julius,* Syd Hoff
16. *Oliver,* Syd Hoff
17. *Sammy the Seal,* Syd Hoff
18. *Stanley,* Syd Hoff (also paperback)

19. *Dinosaur, My Darling,* Edith Hurd
20. *Hurry Hurry,* Edith Hurd
21. *Johnny Lion's Book,* Edith Hurd
22. *Last One Home Is a Green Pig,* Edith Hurd
23. *Harold and the Purple Crayon,* Crockett Jackson
24. *A Picture for Harold's Room,* Crockett Jackson (also paperback)
25. *How the Rooster Saved the Day,* Arnold Lobel
26. *Small Pig,* Arnold Lobel
27. *Father Bear Comes Home,* Else Minarik (also paperback)
28. *Little Bear,* Else Minarik (also paperback)
29. *Little Bear's Friend,* Else Minarik
30. *Little Bear's Visit,* Else Minarik
31. *No Fighting, No Biting!* Else Minarik (also paperback)
32. *Amelia Bedelia and the Surprise Shower,* Peggy Parrish
33. *Morris the Moose Goes to School,* B. Wiseman (also paperback)
34. *Magic Secrets,* Rose Wyler and Gerald Ames (Harper & Row; Scholastic paperback)
35. *Spooky Tricks,* Rose Wyler and Gerald Ames
36. *Harry and the Lady Next Door,* Gene Zion

I. **Harper & Row: I Can Read history books**
1. *George, the Drummer Boy,* Nathaniel Benchley
2. *Sam the Minuteman,* Nathaniel Benchley
3. *Wagon Wheels,* Barbara Brenner
4. *Clipper Ship,* Thomas P. Lewis
5. *Hill of Fire,* Thomas P. Lewis

J. **Harper & Row: I Can Read mystery books**
1. *A Ghost Named Fred,* Nathaniel Benchley
2. *The Strange Disappearance of Arthur Cluck,* Nathaniel Benchley
3. *The Case of the Hungry Stranger,* Crosby Bonsall
4. *The Binky Brothers, Detectives,* James Lawrence

5. *The Binky Brothers and the Fearless Four*, James Lawrence
6. *The Homework Caper*, Joan Lexau

K. **Harper & Row: I Can Read science books**
   1. *Steven and the Green Turtle*, William Cromie
   2. *Look for a Bird*, Edith Hurd
   3. *Ants Are Fun*, Mildred Myrick
   4. *The Penguins Are Coming*, R. L. Penney
   5. *Donald and the Fish That Walked*, Edward Ricciuti
   6. *Greg's Microscope*, Millicent Selsam
   7. *Is This a Baby Dinosaur and Other Science Puzzles*, Millicent Selsam
   8. *Let's Get Turtles*, Millicent Selsam
   9. *More Potatoes!* Millicent Selsam
   10. *Plenty of Fish*, Millicent Selsam
   11. *Seeds and More Seeds*, Millicent Selsam
   12. *Terry and the Caterpillars*, Millicent Selsam
   13. *Tony's Birds*, Millicent Selsam
   14. *When an Animal Grows*, Millicent Selsam
   15. *Fish Out of School*, Evelyn Shaw
   16. *Nest of Wood Ducks*, Evelyn Shaw
   17. *Octopus*, Evelyn Shaw
   18. *Prove It!* Rose Wyler and Gerald Ames

L. **Harper & Row: I Can Read sports books**
   1. *Here Comes the Strikeout*, Leonard Kessler
   2. *Kick, Pass, and Run*, Leonard Kessler
   3. *Last One In Is a Rotten Egg*, Leonard Kessler
   4. *On Your Mark, Get Set, Go!* Leonard Kessler
   5. *Play Ball, Amelia Bedelia*, Peggy Parrish

M. **McGraw-Hill: Science books by Tillie Pine and Joseph Levine**
   1. *Energy All Around*
   2. *Friction All Around*
   3. *Gravity All Around*
   4. *Heat All Around*
   5. *Rocks and How We Use Them*

    6. *Scientists and Their Discoveries*
    7. *Simple Machines and How We Use Them*
    8. *Water All Around*

N. **Other McGraw-Hill science books**
    1. *Investigating Science in the Swimming Pool and Ocean,* Norman Anderson
    2. *Investigating Science Using Your Whole Body,* Norman Anderson
    3. *All Around You,* Jeanne Bendick
    4. *Science Fun with a Flashlight,* Jeanne Bendick
    5. *What Could You See?* Jeanne Bendick
    6. *What Made You?* Jeanne Bendick
    7. *Science Fun for You in a Minute or Two,* Herman and Nina Schneider
    8. *Magnify and Find Out Why,* J. Schwartz

O. **Putnam's: See and Read biography series**
    1. *John Muir,* Glen Dines
    2. *The Great Houdini,* Anne Edwards
    3. *Davy Crockett,* Anne Ford
    4. *Ben Franklin,* Estelle Friedman
    5. *Frederick Douglass,* Charles P. Graves
    6. *The Wright Brothers,* Charles P. Graves
    7. *Theodore Roosevelt,* Sibyl Hancock
    8. *Jacques Cousteau,* Genie Iverson
    9. *Annie Sullivan,* Mary Malone
   10. *Abraham Lincoln,* Patricia Martin
   11. *Daniel Boone,* Patricia Martin
   12. *John Fitzgerald Kennedy,* Patricia Martin
   13. *Pocahontas,* Patricia Martin
   14. *Thomas Alva Edison,* Patricia Martin
   15. *Johnny Appleseed,* Gertrude Norman
   16. *Richard E. Byrd,* Helen Olds
   17. *Buffalo Bill,* Eden Y. Stevens
   18. *George Washington,* Vivian Thompson
   19. *Walt Disney,* Greta Walker

20. *Martin Luther King,* Beth Wilson
21. *Booker T. Washington,* William Wise

P. **Random House: Beginner Books**

1. *The Bear Detectives,* Stanley and Janice Berenstain
2. *The Bears' Christmas,* Stanley and Janice Berenstain
3. *The Bear Scouts,* Stanley and Janice Berenstain
4. *The Bears' Picnic,* Stanley and Janice Berenstain
5. *The Bears' Vacation,* Stanley and Janice Berenstain
6. *The Berenstain Bears Go to School,* Stanley and Janice Berenstain
7. *Inside Outside Upside Down,* Stanley and Janice Berenstain
8. *Animal Riddles,* Bennett Cerf
9. *Book of Laughs,* Bennett Cerf
10. *Book of Riddles,* Bennett Cerf
11. *Babar Loses His Crown,* Jean de Brunhoff
12. *Are You My Mother?* P. D. Eastman
13. *Go Dog Go!* P. D. Eastman
14. *Sam and the Firefly,* P. D. Eastman
15. *Snow,* Roy McKie and P. D. Eastman
16. *The Big Jump,* Benjamin Elkin
17. *The Beginner Book of Things to Make,* Robert Lopshire
18. *Put Me in the Zoo,* Robert Lopshire
19. *A Fish Out of Water,* Helen Palmer
20. *I Was Kissed by a Seal at the Zoo,* Helen Palmer
21. *Why I Built the Boogle House,* Helen Palmer
22. *Hugh Lofting's Doctor Doolittle and the Pirates,* Al Perkins
23. *Hugh Lofting's Travels of Doctor Doolittle,* Al Perkins
24. *Ann Can Fly,* Fred Phleger
25. *Cat's Quizzer,* Dr. Seuss
26. *Dr. Seuss's ABC,* Dr. Seuss
27. *Dr. Seuss's Sleep Book,* Dr. Seuss
28. *Foot Book,* Dr. Seuss

29. *Fox in Socks*, Dr. Seuss. This is an especially good book for a child just learning to read. With it, she can practice phonics in the most painless way possible. Read it to your youngster in the preschool years, and let her read it to you as she is learning to read.
30. *Green Eggs and Ham*, Dr. Seuss
31. *Hop on Pop*, Dr. Seuss
32. *I Can Read with My Eyes Shut!* Dr. Seuss
33. *My Book About Me*, Dr. Seuss
34. *Oh! The Thinks You Can Think*, Dr. Seuss
35. *One Fish, Two Fish, Red Fish, Blue Fish*, Dr. Seuss
36. *Please Try to Remember the First of Octember*, Dr. Seuss
37. *The Cat in the Hat*, Dr. Seuss
38. *The Cat in the Hat Comes Back*, Dr. Seuss

Q. **Franklin Watts: The Let's Find Out books**

1. *Bees*, Cathleen Fitzgerald
2. *Earth*, David Knight
3. *Mars*, David Knight
4. *Telephones*, David Knight
5. *Weather*, David Knight
6. *Frogs*, Corinne Naden
7. *The City*, Valerie Pitt
8. *Communications*, Valerie Pitt
9. *The Family*, Valerie Pitt
10. *Hospitals*, Valerie Pitt
11. *Manners*, Valerie Pitt
12. *Animal Homes*, Martha and Charles Shapp
13. *Babies*, Martha and Charles Shapp
14. *Cavemen*, Martha and Charles Shapp
15. *Indians*, Martha and Charles Shapp
16. *Space Travel*, Martha and Charles Shapp
17. *The Moon*, Martha and Charles Shapp
18. *The Sun*, Martha and Charles Shapp
19. *Water*, Martha and Charles Shapp

20. *What Electricity Does*, Martha and Charles Shapp
21. *What's Big and What's Small*, Martha and Charles Shapp
22. *What's Light and What's Heavy*, Martha and Charles Shapp
23. *Let's Find Out About Christmas*, Franklin Watts
24. *Let's Find Out About Easter*, Franklin Watts
25. *Subtraction*, David Whitney

R.  **Wonder Books Easy Readers series**
1. *Will You Come to My Party?* Sara Asheron
2. *The Monkey in the Rocket*, Jean Bethell
3. *When I Grow Up*, Jean Bethell
4. *Let Papa Sleep*, Crosby Bonsall and E. Reed
5. *Adventures of Silly Billy*, Tamara Kitt
6. *The Boy, the Cat, and the Magic Fiddle*, Tamara Kitt
7. *The Birthday Party*, P. Newman
8. *A Surprise in the Tree*
9. *Jokes and Riddles*
10. *Question and Answer Book*

## II. BOOKS DEALING WITH INTELLECTUAL OR EMOTIONAL DEVELOPMENT

In addition to fostering your child's language development, these books can be read to her to stimulate her general intellectual development. They are categorized according to the particular aspect of development that they deal with. Since some books cannot be categorized precisely, you may find a particular title listed in more than one place.

A.  **Teaching Values and Ethics to Children**
1. *The Value of Caring: Story of Eleanor Roosevelt*, Ann Johnson (Oak Tree Publications)
2. *The Value of Determination: Story of Helen Keller*, Ann Johnson (Oak Tree Publications)

3. *The Value of Responsibility: Story of Ralph Bunche*, Ann Johnson (Oak Tree Publications)
4. *The Value of Believing in Yourself: Story of Louis Pasteur*, Spencer Johnson (Oak Tree Publications)
5. *The Value of Courage: Story of Jackie Robinson*, Spencer Johnson (Oak Tree Publications)
6. *The Value of Curiosity: Story of Christopher Columbus*, Spencer Johnson (Oak Tree Publications)
7. *The Value of Patience: Story of the Wright Brothers*, Spencer Johnson (Oak Tree Publications)
8. *The Value of Saving: Story of Benjamin Franklin*, Spencer Johnson (Oak Tree Publications)

B. **Books About Grandparents**
1. *Grandpa*, Barbara Borack (Harper & Row)
2. *My Grandfather and I*, Helen Buckley (Lothrop, Lee & Shepard)
3. *My Grandmother and I*, Helen Buckley (Lothrop, Lee & Shepard)
4. *Nana Upstairs, Nana Downstairs*, Tomie DePaola (Putnam's; also Penguin paperback)
5. *Watch Out for the Chicken Feet in Your Soup*, Tomie DePaola (Prentice-Hall)
6. *Grandpa's Farm*, James Flora (Harcourt Brace)
7. *Grandpa's Ghost Stories*, James Flora (Atheneum)
8. *My Grandpa Died Today*, Joan Gassler (Human Sciences Press)
9. *Grandpa and Me*, Patricia L. Gauch (Coward, McCann)
10. *Grandma Is Somebody Special*, Susan Goldman (Albert Whitman)
11. *Grandma's Zoo*, Shirley Gordon (Harper & Row)
12. *Grandmother Orphan*, Phyllis Green (Thomas Nelson)
13. *Grandpa's Maria*, Hans-Eric Hellberg (William Morrow)
14. *Grandpa Had a Windmill, Grandma Had a Churn*, Louise Jackson (Parents' Magazine Press)

15. *Grandpa, Me and Our House in the Tree*, Barbara Kirk (Macmillan)
16. *Granny's Fish Story*, Phyllis LaFarge (Parents' Magazine Press)
17. *I Have Four Names for My Grandfather*, Kathryn Lasky (Prentice-Hall)
18. *Grandma's Beach Surprise*, Ilka List (Putnam's)
19. *Why Are There More Questions Than Answers, Grandad?* Kenneth Mahood (Bradbury Press)
20. *Grandfather's Story*, Mervin Marquadt (Concordia)
21. *Simon's Extra Gran*, Pamela Oldfield (A. W. Children's)
22. *I Love My Grandma*, Steven Palay (Raintree Publishers)
23. *Granny and the Baby and the Big Gray Thing*, Peggy Parrish (Macmillan)
24. *Granny and the Desperadoes*, Peggy Parrish (Macmillan; also paperback)
25. *Granny and the Indians*, Peggy Parrish (Macmillan; also paperback)
26. *Grandparents Around the World: Photos from 20 Lands*, Dorka Raynor (Albert Whitman)
27. *Mandy's Grandmother*, Liesel Skorpen (Dial Press)
28. *Grandpa and My Sister Bea*, Joan Tate (A. W. Children's)
29. *Mary Jo's Grandmother*, Janice Udry (Albert Whitman)
30. *Grandmother Told Me*, Jan Wahl (Little, Brown)
31. *Grandpa's Indian Summer*, Jan Wahl and Jeanne Scribner (Prentice-Hall)
32. *Grandmothers*, Glenway Wescott (Atheneum)
33. *Kevin's Grandma*, Barbara Williams (Dutton; also paperback)
34. *Grandmother Lucy Goes on a Picnic*, Joyce Wood (Collins & World)
35. *Grandfathers Are to Love and Grandmothers Are to*

*Love,* boxed set, Lois Wyse (Parents' Magazine Press)

36. *My Grandson Lew,* Charlotte Zolotow (Harper & Row)
37. *William's Doll,* Charlotte Zolotow (Harper & Row)

## C. The Alphabet and Learning to Read

1. *All About Arthur: An Absolutely Absurd Ape,* Eric Carle (Franklin Watts)
2. *I'll Teach My Dog 100 Words,* Dick Gackenbach (Harper & Row)
3. *The Headstart Book of Knowing and Naming,* Shari Lewis and Jacqueline Reinach (McGraw-Hill)
4. *The Magic World of Words* (Macmillan)
5. *Follett's Picture Dictionary* Alta McIntire (Follett)
6. *Pooh's Alphabet Book,* A. A. Milne (Dutton; also Dell paperback)
7. Jane Mocure's Series of Five (Child's World)
   a) *Play with "A" and "T"*
   b) *Play with "E" and "D"*
   b) *Play with "I" and "G"*
   d) *Play with "O" and "G"*
   e) *Play with "U" and "G"*
8. Jane Mocure's Series of Ten (Child's World)
   a) *My "B" Sound Box*
   b) *My "D" Sound Box*
   c) *My "F" Sound Box*
   d) *My "H" Sound Box*
   e) *My "L" Sound Box*
   f) *My "P" Sound Box*
   g) *My "R" Sound Box*
   h) *My "S" Sound Box*
   i) *My "T" Sound Box*
   j) *My "W" Sound Box*
9. *ABC of Monsters,* Deborah Niland (McGraw-Hill)
10. *Alphabrutes,* Dennis Nolan (Prentice-Hall)

11. *Silent E Man: Sesame Street Book of Letters* (Random House)

12. *Alligators All Around,* Maurice Sendak (Harper & Row)

13. *Zag: A Search Through the Alphabet,* Robert Tallon (Holt, Rinehart & Winston)

14. *Loud-Noisy, Dirty-Grimy, Bad and Naughty Twins: A Book of Synonyms,* Sylvia Tester (Child's World)

15. *Never Monkey with a Monkey,* Sylvia Tester (Child's World)

16. *What Did You Say?* Sylvia Tester (Child's World)

D. **Sensory Awareness and Perceptual Acuity**
   1. *My Five Senses,* Aliki (Crowell; also paperback)
   2. *Do You Move as I Do?* Helen Borten (Abelard-Schuman)
   3. *Do You See What I See?* Helen Borten (Abelard-Schuman)
   4. *The Headstart Book of Looking and Listening,* Shari Lewis and Jacqueline Reinach (McGraw-Hill)
   5. *Follow Your Nose,* Paul Showers (Crowell)
   6. *The Listening Walk,* Paul Showers (Crowell)
   7. *Things We Hear,* Anthony Thomas (Franklin Watts)

E. **Concept Formation: Seasons of the Year**
   1. *A Year Is Round,* Joan Walsh Anglund (Harcourt Brace)
   2. *The Bears' Almanac,* Stanley and Janice Berenstain (Random House)
   3. *Sunshine Makes the Seasons,* Franklyn Branley (Crowell)
   4. *Wintertime for Animals,* Margaret Cosgrove (Dodd, Mead)
   5. *Winter Bear,* Ruth Craft (Atheneum)
   6. *All for Fall,* Ethel and Leonard Kessler (Parents' Magazine Press)

7. *Fall Is Here!* Jane Moncure (Child's World)
8. *Spring Is Here!* Jane Moncure (Child's World)
9. *Summer Is Here!* Jane Moncure (Child's World)
10. *Winter Is Here!* Jane Moncure (Child's World)
11. *All Year Long*, Richard Scarry (Western Publishing; also paperback)
12. *Summers Fly, Winters Walk*, Charles Schulz (Holt, Rinehart & Winston)
13. *Let's Find Out About Fall*, Martha and Charles Shapp (Franklin Watts)
14. *Let's Find Out About Spring*, Martha and Charles Shapp (Franklin Watts)
15. *Let's Find Out About Winter*, Martha and Charles Shapp (Franklin Watts)
16. *Summer Is*, Charlotte Zolotow (Abelard-Schuman)

F. **Concept Formation: Comparisons**
1. *High Sounds, Low Sounds*, Franklyn Branley (Crowell; also paperback)
2. *Which Is Bigger?*, Mary Brewer (Child's World)
3. *Playing with Opposites*, Iris Grender (Pantheon paperback)
4. *Push, Pull, Empty, Full: A Book of Opposites*, Tana Hoban (Macmillan; also paperback)
5. *The Very Little Boy*, Phyllis Krasilovsky (Doubleday paperback)
6. *The Very Little Girl*, Phyllis Krasilovsky (Doubleday paperback)
7. *Fast Is Not a Ladybug*, Miriam Schlein (A. W. Children's)
8. *Heavy Is a Hippopotamus*, Miriam Schlein (A. W. Children's)
9. *Over, Under and All Around*, Sylvia Tester (Child's World)
10. *Up Above and Down Below*, Irma Webber (A. W. Children's)
11. *So Big*, Eloise Wilkin (Western Publishing)

G. **Concept Formation: Classification by Shape**
   1. *A Kiss Is Round*, Blossom Budney (Lothrop, Lee & Shepard)
   2. *My Very First Book of Shapes*, Eric Carle (Crowell)
   3. *The Wing on a Flea*, Ed Emberley (Little, Brown)
   4. *Playing with Shapes and Sizes*, Iis Grender (Knopf paperback)
   5. *Circles, Triangles and Squares*, Tana Hoban (Macmillan)
   6. *Shapes and Things*, Tana Hoban (Macmillan)
   7. *Square Is a Shape: A Book About Shapes*, Sharon Lerner (Lerner Publications)
   8. *On My Beach There Are Many Pebbles*, Leo Lionni (Astor-Honor)
   9. *Shapes*, Miriam Schlein (A. W. Children's)
   10. *The Shape of Me and Other Stuff*, Dr. Seuss (Random House)
   11. *Hello, This Is a Shape Book*, John Trotta (Random House)

H. **Concept Formation: Classification by Color**
   1. *Ant and Bee and the Rainbow*, Angela Banner (Franklin Watts)
   2. *The Color Kittens*, Margaret Wise Brown (Western Publishing)
   3. *Let's Find Out about Color*, Ann Campbell (Franklin Watts)
   4. *My Very Best Book of Colors*, Eric Carle (Crowell)
   5. *The Color Factory*, John Denton (Penguin paperback)
   6. *See What I Am*, Roger Duvoisin (Lothrop, Lee & Shepard)
   7. *Green Says Go*, Ed Emberley (Little, Brown)
   8. *What Color Is Your World?*, Bob Fill (Astor-Honor)
   9. *Color Me Brown*, revised edition, Lucille Giles (Johnson Publishing)

10. *Is It Red? Is It Yellow? Is It Blue?*, Tana Hoban (Greenwillow Books)
11. *Orange Is a Color*, Sharon Lerner (Lerner Publications)
12. *A Color of His Own*, Leo Lionni (Pantheon)
13. *Little Blue and Little Yellow*, Leo Lionni (Astor-Honor)
14. *The Great Blueness and Other Predicaments*, Arnold Lobel (Harper & Row)
15. *Richard Scarry's Color Book*, Richard Scarry (Random House)

I. **Concept Formation: Numbers and Counting**
1. *Anno's Counting Book*, Mitsumasa Anno (Crowell)
2. *One, Two, Three with Ant and Bee*, Angela Banner (Franklin Watts)
3. *Berenstain Bears' Counting Book*, Stanley and Janice Berenstain (Random House)
4. *One, Two, Three: An Animal Counting Book*, Margaret Wise Brown (Atlantic Monthly Press)
5. *I Can Count*, Dick Bruna (Methuen)
6. *I Can Count More*, Dick Bruna (Methuen)
7. *Moja Means One: The Swahili Counting Book*, Muriel Feelings (Dial Press paperback)
8. *Ants Go Marching*, Berniece Freschet (Scribner's)
9. *Three by Three*, James Krauss (Macmillan; also paperback)
10. *Ten Little Elephants: A First Counting Book*, Robert Leydenfrost (Doubleday)
11. *10 Bears in My Bed: A Goodnight Countdown*, Stan Mack (Pantheon)
12. *One Is One*, Tasha Tudor (Rand McNally)
13. *One Is No Fun, But Twenty Is Plenty!* Ilse-Margaret Vogel (Atheneum paperback)

J. **Concept Formation: Time**
1. *Do You Know What Time It Is?* Roz Abisch (Prentice-Hall paperback)

2. *Ant and Bee Time,* Angela Banner (Franklin Watts)
3. *What Time Is It Around the World?* Hans Baumann (Scroll Press)
4. *Time and Clocks,* Herta Breiter (Raintree Publishers)
5. *Time and Mr. Bass,* Eleanor Cameron (Little, Brown)
6. *Just a Minute: A Book About Time,* Leonore Klein (Harvey House)
7. *What Time Is It?* John Peter (Grosset & Dunlap)
8. *Time,* Harlan Wade (Raintree Publishers)
9. *Time: A Book to Begin On,* Leslie Waller (Holt, Rinehart & Winston)

K. **Concept Formation: Basic Science Concepts That Tie a Large Number of Events Together in One Concept**

1. *Atoms,* Melvin Berger (Coward, McCann)
2. *Gravity Is a Mystery,* Franklyn Branley (Crowell)
3. *The Fresh Look Series,* J. Curtis (British Book Centre)
   a) *A Fresh Look at Atoms and Molecules* (also paperback)
   b) *A Fresh Look at Evolution*
   c) *A Fresh Look at Gravity*
   d) *A Fresh Look at the Solar System*
   e) *A Fresh Look at Water*
4. *Friction,* Howard Liss (Coward, McCann)
5. *Heat,* Howard Liss (Coward, McCann)
6. *Energy All Around,* Tillie Pine and Joseph Levine (McGraw-Hill)
7. *Friction All Around,* Tillie Pine and Joseph Levine (McGraw-Hill)
8. *Gravity All Around,* Tillie Pine and Joseph Levine (McGraw-Hill)
9. *Heat All Around,* Tillie Pine and Joseph Levine (McGraw-Hill)
10. *Motion,* Seymour Simon (Coward, McCann)

11. *Electricity*, Edward Victor (Follett)
12. *Friction*, Edward Victor (Follett)
13. *Electricity*, Harlan Wade (Raintree Publishers)
14. *Heat*, Harlan Wade (Raintree Publishers)
15. *Levers*, Harlan Wade (Raintree Publishers)
16. *Sound*, Harlan Wade (Raintree Publishers)

L. **Other General Books on Science**

1. *In the Days of the Dinosaurs*, Roy Chapman Andrews (Random House)
2. *Earthquakes*, Charles Cazeau (Follett)
3. *Nature at Its Strangest*, James Comell, Jr. (Sterling)
4. *Where Are You Going with That Energy?*, Roy Doty (Doubleday)
5. *Dr. Beaumont and the Man with the Hole in His Stomach*, Beryl and Samuel Epstein (Coward, McCann)
6. *Nature's Squirt Guns, Bubble Pipes and Fireworks: Geysers, Hot Springs, and Volcanoes*, Alice Gilbreath (David McKay)
7. *Insects Do the Strangest Things*, Leonora and Arthur Hornblow (Random House)
8. *Let's Look at Insects*, Harriet Huntington (Doubleday)
9. *Let's Look at Reptiles*, Harriet Huntington (Doubleday)
10. Lerner Publications: First Fact books
    a) *First Facts About Rockets and Astronauts*, Brenda Thompson and Rosemary Giesen
    b) *First Facts About Animal Attackers*, Brenda Thompson and Cynthia Overbeck
    c) *First Facts About Monkeys and Apes*, Brenda Thompson and Cynthia Overbeck
    d) *First Facts About the Spaceship Earth*, Brenda Thompson and Cynthia Overbeck
    e) *First Facts About Under the Sea*, Brenda Thompson and Cynthia Overbeck
    f) *First Facts About Volcanoes*, Brenda Thompson and Cynthia Overbeck

11. *Animal Habits,* George Mason (William Morrow)
12. *Sounds All About,* Illa Podendorf (A. W. Children's)

M. **The Magic of Words and the Magic of Books**
   1. *Nailheads and Potato Eyes,* Cynthia Basil (William Morrow)
   2. *The Magic Word Book,* An Electric Company book (Random House)
   3. *Beginning Search-a-Word Shapes,* Dawn Gerger (Grosset & Dunlap)
   4. *Watchamacallit Book,* Bernice Hunt (Putnam's)
   5. *What a Funny Thing to Say,* Bernice Kohn (Dial Press)
   6. *Rabbit and Pork: Rhyming Talk,* John Laurence (Crowell)
   7. *The Magic World of Words!* (Macmillan)
   8. *Play on Words,* Alice and Martin Provenson (Random House)
   9. *I Like the Library,* Anne Rockwell (Dutton)
   10. *Fun with Words,* Richard Scarry (Golden Press)
   11. *Books Are Fun,* Geri Shubert (Western Publishing)
   12. *CDB!,* William Steig (Simon & Schuster; also Dutton paperback)

N. **Nonsense Poems**
   Reading nonsense poems aloud is a good way to get a child interested in words and language at an early age. You can begin reading these books to your youngster when he is about four years old.
   1. *Cats and Bats and Things with Wings,* Conrad Aiken (Atheneum)
   2. *Cats and Bats and Things Like That,* Gill Beers (Moody Press)
   3. *Laughable Limericks,* edited by Sara and John Brewton (Crowell)
   4. *Nuts to You and Nuts to Me! An Alphabet of Poems,* Mary Hoberman (Knopf)

5. *At the Top of My Voice*, Felice Holman (Scribner's)
6. *Poetry for Chuckles and Grins*, edited by Leland B. Jacobs (Garrard)
7. *The Book of Nonsense*, Edward Lear (Garland)
8. *Lear's Nonsense Omnibus*, Edward Lear (Frederick Warne)
9. *The Nutcrackers and the Sugar-Tongs*, Edward Lear (Little, Brown)
10. *The Owl and the Pussycat*, Edward Lear (Atheneum; also paperback)
11. *The Pobble Who Has No Toes and Other Nonsense*, Edward Lear (Viking Press)
12. *Alligator Pie*, Dennis Lee (Houghton Mifflin)
13. *The Scroobious Pip*, Edward Lear, completed by Ogden Nash (Harper & Row)
14. *Dinosaur Do's and Don'ts*, Jean Polhamus (Prentice-Hall)
15. *A Great Big Ugly Man Came Up and Tied His Horse to Me: A Book of Nonsense Verse*, Wallace Tripp (Little, Brown)
16. *Giant Poems*, edited by Daisy Wallace (Holiday House)
17. *Father Fox's Pennyrhymes*, Clyde Watson (Scholastic paperback)

O. **Problem-Solving**

1. *Why: A Book of Reasons*, Irving and Ruth Adler (John Day)
2. *Why and How: A Second Book of Reasons*, Irving and Ruth Adler (John Day)
3. *Why Can't I?* Jeanne Bendick (McGraw-Hill)
4. *What Makes Day and Night?* Franklyn Branley (Crowell; also paperback)
5. *What Makes a Shadow?* Clyde Bulla (Crowell)
6. *The Shadow Book*, Beatrice DeRegniers (Harcourt Brace)
7. *What Can You Do with a Shoe?* Beatrice DeRegniers (Harper & Row)

8. *Are You My Mother?* P. D. Eastman (Beginner Books)
9. *Why Didn't I Think of That?* Web Garrison (Prentice-Hall)
10. *Sometimes I Worry*, Alan Gross (A. W. Children's)
11. *Up Day, Down Day*, Jacquie Hann (Four Winds Press)
12. *What Would You Do?* Leland Jacobs (Garrard)
13. *What If I Couldn't: A Book About Special Needs*, Janet Kamien (Scribner's)
14. *Help!* Susan Riley (Child's World)
15. *Mom's New Job*, Paul Sawyer (Raintree Publishers)

P. **Children's Emotions or Special Problems**
1. *I Feel*, George Ancona (Dutton)
2. *Love Is a Special Way of Feeling*, Joan Walsh Anglund (Harcourt Brace)
3. *I Have Feelings*, Terry Berger (Human Sciences Press)
4. *The Dead Bird*, Margaret Wise Brown (A. W. Children's)
5. *Will I Have a Friend?* Miriam Cohen (Macmillan; also paperback)
6. *I Dare You!* Judith Conaway (Raintree Publishers)
7. *I'll Get Even*, Judith Conaway (Raintree Publishers)
8. *Sometimes It Scares Me*, Judith Conaway (Raintree Publishers
9. *Was My Face Red*, Judith Conaway (Raintree Publishers)
10. *Will I Ever Be Good Enough?* Judith Conaway (Raintree Publishers)
11. *Feelings Between Kids and Grown-ups*, Marcia Conta and Maureen Reardon (Raintree Publishers)
12. *Feelings Between Kids and Parents*, Marcia Conta and Maureen Reardon (Raintree Publishers)
13. *All Alone with Daddy*, Joan Fassler (Human Sciences Press)

14. *The Boy with a Problem*, Joan Fassler (Human Sciences Press)
15. *Don't Worry, Dear*, Joan Fassler (Human Sciences Press)
16. *The Man of the House*, Joan Fassler (Human Sciences Press)
17. *My Grandpa Died Today*, Joan Fassler (Human Sciences Press)
18. *Where Is Daddy? A Story of Divorce*, Beth Goff (Beacon Press)
19. *I Won't Be Afraid*, Joan Hanson (Carolrhoda Books)
20. *I'm Running Away*, Ann Helena (Raintree Publishers)
21. *Lie*, Ann Helena (Raintree Publishers)
22. *That Makes Me Mad!*, Steven Kroll (Pantheon)
23. *Emily and the Klunky Baby and the Next Door Dog*, Joan Lexau (Dial Press)
24. *Me Day*, Joan Lexau (Dial Press)
25. *Mommy and Daddy Are Divorced*, Patricia Perry (Dial Press)
26. *Curious George Goes to the Hospital*, Margaret and H. A. Rey (Houghton Mifflin)
27. *Angry*, Susan Riley (A. W. Children's)
28. *Mom's New Job*, Paul Sawyer (Raintree Publishers)
29. *Dentist and Me*, Joy Schaleben-Lewis (Raintree Publishers)
30. *Gorilla in the Hall*, Alice Schertle (Lothrop, Lee & Shepard)
31. *I Hate It*, Miriam Schlein (Albert Whitman)
32. *I Don't Care*, Marjorie Sharmatt (Macmillan)
33. *Sometimes I Like to Cry*, Elizabeth and Henry Stanton (Albert Whitman)
34. *My Mama Says There Aren't Any Zombies, Ghosts, Vampires, Creatures, Demons, Monsters, Fiends, Goblins, or Things*, Judith Viorst (Atheneum paperback)

35. *The Tenth Good Thing About Barney* Judith Viorst (Atheneum paperback)
36. *Sometimes I Get Angry,* Jane W. Watson (Western Publishing; also paperback)
37. *Sometimes I'm Afraid,* Jane W. Watson (Western Publishing; also paperback)
38. *Sometimes I'm Jealous,* Jane W. Watson (Western Publishing; also paperback)
39. *Timid Timothy,* Gweneira Williams (A. W. Children's)
40. *This Room Is Mine,* Betty Wright (Western Publishing)
41. *Big Sister and Little Sister,* Charlotte Zolotow (Harper & Row)
42. *The Hating Book,* Charlotte Zolotow (Harper & Row)
43. *The Quarreling Book,* Charlotte Zolotow (Harper & Row)

**Q. Mathematics**

1. *The True Book of Metric Measurement,* June Behrens (A. W. Children's)
2. *How Little and How Much? A Book About Scales,* Franklyn Branley (Crowell)
3. *Measure with Metric,* Franklyn Branley (Crowell; also paperback)
4. *About the Metric System,* Alma Filleo (Child's World)
5. *The Greatest Guessing Game: A Book About Dividing,* Robert Froman (Crowell)
6. *Count and See,* Tana Hoban (Macmillan)
7. *Metric Can Be Fun,* Munro Leaf (Lippincott; also paperback)
8. Series of six books by Vincent O'Connor (Raintree Child)
   a) *Mathematics at the Farm*
   b) *Mathematics in Buildings*

      c) *Mathematics in the Circus Ring*
      d) *Mathematics in the Kitchen*
      e) *Mathematics in the Toy Store*
      f) *Mathematics on the Playground*

9. *Humphrey, the Number Horse,* Rodney Peppe (Viking Press)
10. *Numbers, Signs and Pictures: A First Number Book,* Shari Robinson (Platt & Munk)
11. *How Did Numbers Begin?* Mindel and Harry Sitomer (Crowell)
12. *Zero Is Not Nothing,* Harry and Mindel Sitomer (Crowell)
13. *Solomon Grundy, Born On One Day: A Finite Arithmetic Book,* Malcolm Weiss (Crowell)
14. *Let's Find Out About Subtraction,* David Whitney (Franklin Watts)

R. **Scientific Methods for Preschoolers**
1. *The Smallest Life Around Us,* Lucia Anderson (Crown)
2. *What Could You See?* Jeanne Bendick (McGraw-Hill)
3. *Berenstain Bears' Science Fair,* Stanley and Janice Berenstain (Random House)
4. *How Can I Find Out?* Mary Bongiorno and Mable Gee (Children's Press)
5. *The Real Magnet Book,* Mae Freeman (Scholastic paperback)
6. *The Headstart Book of Thinking and Imagining,* Shari Lewis and Jacqueline Reinach (McGraw-Hill)
7. *ABC Science Experiments,* Harry Milgrom (Macmillan paperback)
8. *Adventures with a Cardboard Tube,* Harry Milgrom (Dutton)
9. *Simple Science Fun: Experiments with Light, Sound, Air and Water,* Bob Ridiman (Parents' Magazine Press)

10. *Got a Minute? Quick Science Experiments You Can Do,* Nina Schneider (Scholastic paperback)
11. *Magnify and Find Out Why,* J. Schwartz (McGraw-Hill)
12. *Benny's Animals and How He Put Them in Order,* Millicent Selsam (Harper & Row)
13. *Greg's Microscope,* Millicent Selsam (Harper & Row)
14. *Finding Out with Your Senses,* Seymour Simon (McGraw-Hill)
15. *Look! How Your Eyes See,* Marcel Sislowitz (Coward, McCann)
16. *Prove It!* Rose Wyler and Gerald Ames (Harper & Row)

## S. Books About Religion

Sad to say, good books about religion for preschoolers are mighty scarce. Here are a few, but there should be more.

1. *Told Under the Christmas Tree,* Association for Childhood Education International (Macmillan)
2. *Mitzvah Is Something Special,* Phyllis Eisenberg (Harper & Row)
3. *A Book About God,* Florence Fitch (Lothrop, Lee & Shepard)
4. Books by Mary Alice Jones.
   Mrs. Jones has written a series of excellent books on religion for children. Highly recommended. (Rand McNally paperbacks)
   a) *Tell Me About God*
   b) *Tell Me About Jesus*
   c) *Know Your Bible*
5. *Children's Prayers for Today,* Audrey McKim and Dorothy Logan (Association Press)
6. *Wineglass: A Passover Story,* Norman Rosten (Walker & Co.)

T. **The Self-Concept**
1. *My Five Senses,* Aliki (Crowell; also paperback)
2. *My Hands,* Aliki (Crowell)
3. *How I Feel,* June Behrens (A. W. Children's)
4. *Hooray for Me!* Remy Charlip and Lillian Moore (Parents' Magazine Press)
5. *The Boy with the Special Face,* Barbara Girion (Abingdon Press)
6. *Katie's Magic Glasses,* Jane Goodsell (Houghton Mifflin)
7. *To Be Me,* Barbara Hazen (Child's World)
8. *Any Me I Want to Be,* Karla Kaskin (Harper & Row)
9. *About Me,* Jane Moncure (Child's World)
10. *All by Myself,* Jane Moncure (Child's World)
11. *Who Am I?* A Sesame Street book (Western Publishing)
12. *My Book About Me,* Dr. Seuss (Beginner Books)
13. *But Names Will Never Hurt Me,* Bernard Waber (Houghton Mifflin)
14. *Look at Me Now,* Jane Watson (Western Publishing)
15. *What's Inside Me?* Herbert Zim (William Morrow)

U. **Relationsips Within the Family and with Peers**
1. *Without Hats, Who Can Tell the Good Guys?* Mildred Ames (Dutton)
2. *The Terrible Thing That Happened at Our House,* Marge Blaine (Parents' Magazine Press)
3. *It's Mine: A Greedy Book,* Crosby Bonsall (Harper & Row)
4. *Daddy,* Jeanette Caines (Lothrop, Lee & Shepard)
5. *Daddies,* L. C. Carton (Random House)
6. *Mommies,* L. C. Carton (Random House)
7. *Never Is a Long, Long Time,* Dick Cate (Thomas Nelson)

8. *Feelings Between Brothers and Sisters*, Maria Conta and Maureen Reardon (Raintree Publishers)

9. *Feelings Between Friends*, Marcia Conta and Maureen Reardon (Raintree Publishers)

10. *Feelings Between Kids and Parents*, Marcia Conta and Marueen Reardon (Raintree Publishers)

11. *The Little Girl and Her Mother*, Beatrice DeRegniers and Esther Gilman (Vanguard Press)

12. *Humbug Mountain*, Sid Fleischman (Little, Brown)

13. *My Daddy Is a Cool Dude*, Karama and Mahiri Fukama (Dial Press)

14. *Aunt Bernice*, Jack Gantos (Houghton Mifflin)

15. *Family Scrapbook*, M. B. Goffstein (Farrar, Straus & Giroux)

16. *Cousins Are Special*, Susan Goldman (Albert Whitman)

17. *She Come Bringing Me That Little Baby Girl*, Eloise Greenfield (Lippincott)

18. *Animal Babies*, Arthur Gregor (Harper & Row)

19. *We're Very Good Friends, My Brother and I*, P. K. Hallinan (A. W. Children's)

20. *I'm Going to Run Away*, Joan Hansen (Platt & Munk)

21. *Gorilla Wants to Be the Baby*, Barbara Hazen (Atheneum)

22. *Why Couldn't I Be an Only Kid Like You, Wigger?* Barbara Hazen (Atheneum)

23. *My Sister*, Karen Hirsh (Carolrhoda Books)

24. *Confessions of an Only Child*, Norma Klein (Pantheon; also paperback)

25. *It's Okay If You Don't Love Me*, Norma Klein (Dial Press)

26. *When I Grow Up*, Lois Lenski (Henry Z. Walck)

27. *But What About Me?*, Sandra Love (Harcourt Brace)

28. *The Ultra-Violet Catastrophe*, Margaret Mahy (Parents' Magazine Press; also paperback)

29. *My Dad Lives in a Downtown Hotel*, Peggy Mann (Doubleday; also Avon paperbck)
30. *Mommies at Work*, Eve Merriam (Knopf; also Scholastic paperback)
31. *My Daddy Don't·Go to Work*, Madeena Nolan (Carolrhoda Books)
32. *Mommies Are for Loving*, Ruth Penn (Putnam's)
33. *Daddies: What They Do All Day*, Helen Puner (Lothrop, Lee & Shepard)
34. *The Way Mothers Are*, Miriam Schlein (Albert Whitman)
35. *My Family*, Felicity Sen (Bradbury Press)
36. *I Want Mama*, Marjorie Sharmatt (Harper & Row)
37. *Me and My Family Tree*, Paul Showers (Crowell)
38. *Somebody Else's Child*, Roberta Silman (Frederick Warne)
39. *Friday Night Is Papa Night*, Ruth A. Sonneborn (Viking Press)
40. *My Daddy Is a Monster—Sometimes*, John Steptoe (Lippincott)
41. *It's Not Fair*, Robyn Supraner (Frederick Warne)
42. *How Your Mother and Father Met and What Happened After*, Tobi Tobias (McGraw-Hill)
43. *Couldn't We Have a Turtle Instead?* Judith Vigna (Albert Whitman)
44. *Alexander and the Terrible, Horrible No-Good, Very Bad Day*, Judith Viorst (Atheneum)
45. *Julia and the Third Bad Thing*, Barbara Wallace (Follett)
46. *If It Weren't for You*, Charlotte Zolotow (Harper & Row)
47. *When I Have a Little Girl*, Charlotte Zolotow (Harper & Row)
48. *When I Have a Son*, Charlotte Zolotow (Harper & Row)

V. **The Community and Community Helpers**
1. *I Know a Dentist*, Naomi Barnett (Putnam's)

2. *I Know a Nurse*, Marilyn Schima and Polly Bolian (Putnam's)

3. *Clean Streets, Clean Water, Clean Air*, Cynthia Chapin (Albert Whitman)

4. *I Know a Plumber*, Polly Curren (Putnam's)

5. *I Know a Bus Driver*, Genevieve Gray (Putnam's)

6. *Policemen and Firemen: What They Do*, Carla Greene (Harper & Row)

7. *Truck Drivers: What They Do*, Carla Greene (Harper & Row)

8. *I Know a Grocer*, Lorraine Henriod (Putnam's)

9. *I Know a Zoo Keeper*, Lorraine Henriod (Putnam's)

10. *Let's Find Out About Hospitals*, Eleanor Kay (Franklin Watts)

11. *Ask Me What My Mother Does*, Katherine Leiner (Franklin Watts)

12. *Jobs People Do*, Jane Moncure (Child's World)

13. *People Who Help People*, Jane Moncure (Child's World)

14. *People in Your Neighborhood*, Jeffrey Moss (Western Publishing)

15. *Let's Find Out About Neighbors*, Valerie Pitt (Franklin Watts)

16. *Nothing Ever Happens on My Block*, Ellen Raskin (Atheneum)

17. *Butcher, Baker, Cabinetmaker*, Wendy Saul (Crowell)

18. *Busy Town, Busy People*, Richard Scarry (Random House)

19. *Richard Scarry's Busiest People Ever*, Richard Scarry (Random House paperback)

20. *Who Are the People in Yur Neighborhood?* a Sesame Street book (Random House)

21. *Let's Find Out About Firemen*, Martha and Charles Shapp (Franklin watts)

22. *I Know an Airline Pilot*, Muriel Stanek (Putnam's)

23. *I Know a Librarian,* Virginia Voight (Putnam's)
24. *I Know a Fireman,* Barbara Williams (Putnam's)
25. *I Know a Policeman,* Barbara Williams (Putnam's)

W. **The Larger Community: The World**

1. *A Book of Astronauts for You,* Franklyn Branley (Crowell)
2. *A Book of Outer Space for You,* Franklyn Branley (Crowell)
3. *A Book of Planet Earth for You,* Franklyn Branley (Crowell)
4. *You Will Go to the Moon,* Mae and Ira Freeman (Random House)
5. *Children Everywhere,* David Harrison (Rand McNally)
6. *Where in the World Do You Live?* Al Hine and John Alcorn (Harcourt Brace)
7. *The World We Live in,* Arkady Leokum (Grosset & Dunlap)
8. *The World Is Round,* Anthony Ravielli (Viking Press)
9. *Space: A Fact and Riddle Book,* Jane Sharnoff and Reginold Ruffanis (Scribner's)

X. **Richard Scarry**

Richard Scarry is so unique he deserves a category all to himself. He has a series of enchanting books that teach children about the world and the people who live in it. I advise buying a number of these books for your child. He will use them for years and receive enormous intellectual stimulation from them.

1. *All About Animals* (Western Publishing)
2. *All Day Long* (Western Publishing)
3. *Animal Nursery Tales* (Western Publishing)
4. *At Work* (Western Publishing)
5. *Busy, Busy World* (Western Publishing)
6. *Fun with Words* (Golden Press)
7. *Going Places* (Western Publishing)

8. *Hop Aboard, Here We Go!* (Western Publishing)
9. *My House* (Western Publishing)
10. *Nicky Goes to the Doctor* (Western Publishing)
11. *On the Farm* (Western Publishing)
12. *On Vacation* (Western Publishing)
13. *Rabbit and His Friends* (Western Publishing)
14. *Richard Scarry's ABC Word Book* (Random House)
15. *Richard Scarry's Best Counting Book Ever* (Random House)
16. *Richard Scarry's Best Mother Goose Ever* (Western Publishing)
17. *Richard Scarry's Best Storybook Ever* (Western Publishing)
18. *Richard Scarry's Best Word Book Ever* (Western Publishing)
19. *Richard Scarry's Busiest People Ever* (Random House paperback)
20. *Richard Scarry's Cars and Trucks and Things That Go* (Western Publishing)
21. *Richard Scarry's Egg-in-the-Hole Book* (Western Publishing)
22. *Richard Scarry's Favorite Mother Goose Rhymes* (Random House)
23. *Richard Scarry's Find Your ABC's* (Random House)
24. *Richard Scarry's Great Big Air Book* (Random House)
25. *Richard Scarry's Great Big Mystery Book* (Random House)
26. *Richard Scarry's Great Big Schoolhouse* (Random House)
27. *Richard Scarry's Just for Fun* (Golden Press)
28. *Richard Scarry's Please and Thank You Book* (Random House)
29. *Richard Scarry's Postman Pig and His Busy Neighbors* (Random House)
30. *Richard Scarry's Silly Stories* (Random House)

31. *Storybook Dictionary* (Western Publishing)
32. *Things to Know* (Western Publishing)
33. *Things to Learn* (Western Publishing)

## III. FICTION AND FANTASY

1. *The Brave Cowboy*, Joan Walsh Anglund (Harcourt Brace paperback)
2. *Anno's Journey*, Mitsumasa Anno (Collins & World)
3. *Old MacDonald Had an Apartment House*, Judith Barrett (Atheneum paperback)
4. *The Other Way to Listen*, Byrd Baylor (Scribner's)
5. *Madeline*, Ludwig Bemelmans (Viking Press; also Penguin paperback)
6. *The Five Chinese Brothers*, Claire Bishop (Coward, McCann)
7. *Switch on the Night*, Ray Bradbury (Pantheon)
8. *The Snowman*, Raymond Briggs (Random House)
9. *Where Have You Been?* Margaret Wise Brown (Hastings House)
10. *The Story of Babar; Babar and His Children; Babar the King;* and other Babar books, by Jean de Brunhoff (Random House)
11. *Time to Get Out of the Bath, Shirley*, John Burningham (Crowell)
12. *The Little House*, Virginia Burton (Houghton Mifflin; also paperback)
13. *Mike Mulligan and His Steam Shovel*, Virginia Burton (Houghton Mifflin paperback)
14. *Go and Hush the Baby*, Betsy Byars (Viking Press)
15. *Don't You Remember?*, Lucille Clifton (Dutton)
16. *"Bee My Valentine!"* Miriam Cohen (Greenwillow Books)
17. *Timothy Turtle*, Alice Davis (Harcourt Brace; also paperback)

18. *A Little House of Our Own*, Beatrice Schenk DeRegniers and Irene Haas (Harcourt Brace)
19. *May I Bring a Friend?*, Beatrice Schenk DeRegniers (Atheneum; also paperback)
20. *The Alligator Case*, William Pene DuBois (Harper & Row)
21. *Martin's Father*, Margaret Eickler (Lollipop Power Press paperback)
22. *Gilberto and the Wind*, Marie Ets (Viking Press; also Penguin paperback)
23. *The Happy Lion*, Louise Fatio (McGraw-Hill)
24. *Casey, the Utterly Impossible Horse*, Anita Feagles (Scholastic paperback)
25. *Angus and the Cat*, Marjorie Flack (Doubleday; also paperback)
26. *Corduroy*, Don Freeman (Viking Press; also Penguin paperback)
27. *A Rainbow of My Own*, Don Freeman (Viking Press; also paperback)
28. *Little Toot*, Hardie Gramatky (Putnam's; also paperback)
29. *Happy Birthday, Sam*, Pat Hutchins (Greenwillow Books)
30. *Staying Home Alone on a Rainy Day*, Chihiro Iwasaki (McGraw-Hill)
31. *Harold and the Purple Crayon*, Crockett Johnson (Harper & Row)
32. *The Snowy Day*, Ezra Jack Keats (Viking Press; also paperback)
33. *A Hole Is to Dig*, Ruth Krauss (Harper & Row)
34. *Mothers Can Do Anything*, Joe Lasker (Albert Whitman)
35. *Little Pear*, Eleanor Lattimore (Harcourt Brace; also paperback)
36. *The Story of Ferdinand*, Munro Leaf (Viking Press)
37. *The Little Auto*, Lois Lenski (Henry Z. Walck)
38. *Olaf Reads*, Joan Lexau (Dial Press)

39. *Of Course Polly Can Ride a Bike*, Astrid Lindgren (Follett)
40. *The Biggest House in the World*, Leo Lionni (Pantheon; also paperback)
41. *Frederick*, Leo Lionni (Pantheon; also paperback)
42. *Inch by Inch*, Leo Lionni (Astor-Honor)
43. *Theodore Turtle*, Ellen MacGregor (McGraw-Hill)
44. *Blueberries for Sal*, Robert McCloskey (Viking Press; also Penguin paperback)
45. *Burt Dow, Deep Water Man*, Robert McCloskey (Viking Press)
46. *Lentil*, Robert McCloskey (Viking Press, also Penguin paperback)
47. *Make Way for Ducklings*, Robert McCloskey (Viking Press)
48. *One Morning in Maine*, Robert McCloskey (Viking Press)
49. *Frederick's Alligator*, Esther Peterson (Crown)
50. *Little Leo*, Leo Politi (Scribner's)
51. *Pedro, the Angel of Olvera Street*, Leo Politi (Scribner's)
52. *Spectacles*, Ellen Raskin (Atheneum paperback)
53. *Firegirl*, Gibson Rich (Feminist Press paperback)
54. *My Doctor*, Harlow Rockwell (Macmillan)
55. *Rain Makes Applesauce*, Julian Scheer (Holiday House)
56. *Where the Wild Things Are*, Maurice Sendak (Harper & Row)
57. *And to Think That I Saw It on Mulberry Street*, Dr. Seuss (Vanguard Press)
58. *The 500 Hats of Bartholomew Cubbins*, Dr. Seuss (Vanguard Press)
59. *Horton Hatches the Egg*, Dr. Seuss (Random House)
60. *Caps for Sale*, Esphyr Slobodkina (A. W. Children's; also Scholastic paperback)
61. *Anatole*, Eve Titus (McGraw-Hill)
62. *Space Cat*, Ruthven Todd (Scribner's; also paperback)
63. *A Tree Is Nice*, Janice Udry (Harper & Row)

64. *Crictor*, Tomi Ungerer (Harper & Row; also Scholastic paperback)
65. *Emile*, Tomi Ungerer (Harper & Row)
66. *I'll Fix Anthony*, Judith Viorst (Harper & Row)
67. *The House on East 88th Street*, Bernard Waber (Houghton Mifflin; also paperback)
68. *The Biggest Bear*, Lynd Ward (Houghton Mifflin; also paperback)
69. *Crow Boy*, Taro Yashima (Viking Press; also Penguin paperback)
70. *The Summer Night*, Charlotte Zolotow (Harper & Row)

## IV. COLLECTIONS OF STORIES, TALES, OR FOLKTALES

1. *Joan Walsh Anglund Storybook*, Joan Walsh Anglund (Random House)
2. *Told Under the City Umbrella* and *Told Under the Magic Umbrella*, Association for Childhood Education International (Macmillan)
3. *Told Under the Green Imbrella*, Association for Childhood Education International (Macmillan)
4. *Castles and Dragons: Read-to-Yourself Fairy Tales for Boys and Girls*, compiled by the Child Study Association of America (Crowell)
5. *The Book of Greek Myths*, Edgar and Ingri D'Aulaire (Doubleday)
6. *Kate Greenaway Treasury*, Kate Greenaway (Collins & World)
7. *Night Noises and Other Mole and Troll Stories*, Tony Johnson (Putnam's)
8. *I Can Choose My Bedtime Story*, edited by Mary Parsley (Grosset & Dunlap)
9. *Fables of Aesop*, edited by Ruth Spriggs (Rand McNally)
10. *With a Deep Sea Smile*, Virginia Tashjian (Little, Brown)

11. *Storybook: A Collection of Stories Old and New*, compiled by Tomi Ungerer (Franklin Watts)

## V. POETRY FOR PRESCHOOLERS

1. *Sung Under the Silver Umbrella*, Association for Childhood Educational International (Macmillan)
2. *Nibble, Nibble*, Margaret Wise Brown (A. W. Children's)
3. *I Can't, Said the Ant*, Polly Cameron (Coward, Mc-Cann)
4. *I Met a Man*, John Ciardi (Houghton Mifflin; also paperback)
5. *You Read to Me, I'll Read to You*, John Ciardi (Lippincott)
6. *Something Special*, Beatrice Schenk DeRegniers and Irene Haas (Harcourt Brace)
7. *Cricket in a Thicket*, Aileen Fisher (Scribner's; also paperback)
8. *Listen, Children, Listen: An Anthology of Poems for the Very Young*, edited by Myra Cohn Livingston (Harcourt Brace)
9. *When We Were Very Young* and *Now We Are Six*, A. A. Milne (Dutton; also Dell paperback)
10. *What Do You Feed Your Donkey On? Rhymes from a Belfast Childhood*, compiled by Colette O'Hare (Collins & World)
11. *Hailstones and Halibut Bones*, Mary O'Neill (Doubleday; also paperback)
12. *Where the Sidewalk Ends: Poems and Drawings*, Shel Silverstein (Harper & Row)
13. *A Child's Garden of Verses*, Robert Louis Stevenson (Franklin Watts)
14. *Other Books of Poetry*

a) *Make a Circle, Keep Us In: Poems for a Good Day*, Arnold Adoff (Delacorte Press)
b) *A Bunch of Poems and Verses*, Beatrice Schenk De-Regniers (Seabury Press)
c) *Honey, I Love and Other Poems*, Eloise Greenfield (Crowell)
d) *Fat Polka-Dot Cat and Other Haiku*, Betsy Maestro (Dutton)
e) *Flower Moon Snow: A Book of Haiku*, Kazue Mizumura (Crowell)
f) *Poems Make Pictures, Pictures Make Poems*, G. Rimanelli and Paul Rinsleur (Pantheon)
g) *First Poems of Childhood*, Tasha Tudor (Platt & Munk)

## VI. NONSEXIST PICTURE BOOKS

If children are going to grow up to be successful and complete human beings, they need to think of themselves and others in free, unstereotyped, nonsexist ways.

How can you help them to do this? First, you can read nonsexist books to them—books that are not contaminated by the old sexist stereotypes. In this section and the next, I provide you with the titles of a number of very good books that are excellent and truly nonsexist.

Some feminists think you should read only completely nonsexist books to your children, and ignore any books that are tinged even in the slightest by sexism. I disagree. Many very good books listed in this Appendix, particularly the older ones, are sexist. My suggestion is this: If a book is good, read it to your child. If the book is also sexist, point that out and tell him, for example, that the book is mistaken when it implies that it's bad for boys to cry, or that girls should be quiet and submissive.

1. *Mary Alice, Operator Number Nine*, Jeffrey Allen (Little, Brown; also Penguin paperback)
2. *I'm Bored, Ma!*, Harold Berson (Crown)
3. *Bodies*, Barbara Brenner (Dutton)
4. *The Steamroller*, Margaret Wise Brown (Walker & Co.)
5. *Will I Have a Friend?*, Miriam Cohen (Macmillan; also paperback)
6. *Dorrie and the Amazing Elixir*, Patricia Coombs (Lothrop, Lee & Shepard)
7. *Grownups Cry, Too*, Nancy Hazen (Lollipop Power Press)
8. *Max*, Rachael Isadora (Macmillan)
9. *Louie*, Ezra Jack Keats (Greenwillow Books)
10. *Lucky Wilma*, Wendy Kindred (Dial Press)
11. *Monkey Day*, Ruth Krauss (Bookstore Press)
12. *A Bedtime Story*, Joan Goldman Levine (Dutton)
13. *A Wise Monkey Tale*, Betsy Maestro (Crown)
14. *My Mother the Mail-Carrier*, Inez Maury (Feminist Press; also paperback)
15. *Around and Around Love*, Betty Miles (Knopf; also paperback)
16. *Swinging and Swinging*, Fran Manushkin (Harper & Row)
17. *My Nursery School*, Harlow Rockwell (Greenwillow Books)
18. *Morris and His Brave Lion*, Helen Spelman Rogers (McGraw-Hill)
19. *The Wizard's Tears*, Anne Sexton and Maxine Kermin (McGraw-Hill)
20. *I Am a Giant*, Ivan Sherman (Harcourt Brace)
21. *My Special Best Words*, John Steptoe (Viking Press)
22. *Kevin's Grandma*, Barbara Williams (Dutton; also paperback)
23. *Betsy and the Chicken Pox*, Gunilla Wolde (Random House)
24. *The Summer Night*, Charlotte Zolotow (Harper & Row)

## VII. NONSEXIST EASY READERS

This is a group of easy-to-read books that will help your child to transcend the limitations of traditional sex-role stereotypes.

1. *The Most Delicious Camping Trip Ever*, Alice Bach (Harper & Row; also paperback)
2. *I'd Rather Stay Home*, Carol Barkin and Elizabeth James (Raintree Publishers)
3. *He Bear, She Bear*, Stanley and Janice Berenstain (Random House)
4. *And I Mean It, Stanley*, Crosby Bonsall (Harper & Row)
5. *Is This Your Sister? A True Story About Adoption*, Catherine and Sherry Bunin (Pantheon)
6. *Animal Fathers*, Russell Freedman (Holiday House)
7. *Did the Sun Shine Before You Were Born?* Sol Gordon and Judith Cohen (Okpaku Productions)
8. *Delilah*, Carole Hart (Harper & Row)
9. *New Life: New Room*, June Jordan (Crowell)
10. *Fiona's Bee*, Beverly Keller (Coward, McCann; also Dell paperback)
11. *The Missing Piece*, Shel Silverstein (Harper & Row)
12. *All Kinds of Families*, Norman Simon (Albert Whitman)
13. *Eliza's Daddy*, Ianthe Thomas (Harcourt Brace; also paperback)

## VIII. GAME BOOKS

Preschool-age children love games of any kind. These books offer a treasure trove of games that you can play with them. Many of them can be played when you travel, too, and that is a special boon.

1. *A Hole, a Box and a Stick*, Gladys Y. Cretan (Lothrop, Lee & Shepard)

2. *Little Boy Blue: Finger Plays Old and New*, Daphne Hogstrom (Golden Press)
3. *Jack Kent's Hop, Skip and Jump Book*, Jack Kent (Random House; also paperback)
4. *Finger Plays for Nursery and Kindergarten*, Emilie Poulssen (Dover Publications paperback)
5. *Two Hundred Two Things to Do*, Margaret Sedlied (Regal Press; also paperback)

## IX. MISCELLANEOUS

A. **Cooking for Young Children**
   1. *Teddybears' Cookbook*, Susanna Greta (Doubleday)
   2. *Cool Cooking*, Esther Hautzig (Lothrop, Lee & Shepard)
   3. *Kids Cooking Without a Stove: A Cookbook for Young Children*, Aileen Paul (Doubleday)
   4. *Kids Cooking: A First Cookbook for Children*, Aileen Paul and Arthur Hawkins (Archway paperback)
   5. *I Am a Cookbook*, Em Riggs and Barbara Darpinion (J. P. Tarcher)

B. **"Open Books" for Adults and Children**
   These books by Sara Stein have a story that can be read aloud to a child, and a text running beside the story for the parents. This text explains the childhood fears that are being dealt with in the story, the questions a child might have at a given point, and how an adult can further explore the story with the child through questions and discussion. (Walker & Co.)
   1. *A Hospital Story*
   2. *About Dying*
   3. *Making Babies*
   4. *That New Baby*
   5. *Who'll Take Care of Me?*

C. **Western Publishing Read-Together Paperback Books**
This is another series of books specially designed for
parents to read aloud to their preschoolers. The authors are Jane Werner Watson, Dr. R. E. Switzer, and
Dr. J. C. Hirschberg. (Western Publishing)
  1. *My Body—How It Works*
  2. *My Friend, the Babysitter*
  3. *Sometimes I Get Angry*
  4. *Sometimes I'm Afraid*
  5. *Sometimes I'm Jealous*

# NOTES

1. George Gallup, *The Miracle Ahead* (New York: Harper & Row, 1964) c. 1964 by George Gallup.
2. Ibid.
3. Ibid.
4. Paul Copperman, *Literacy Hoax* (New York: William Morrow & Co., 1978).
5. Ibid.
6. Ibid.
7. Ibid.
8. Rudolph Flesch, *Why Johnny Can't Read* (New York: Harper & Row, 1955).
9. Ibid.
10. Richard Zaner and Don Ihde, *Phenomenology and Existentialism* (New York: G. P. Putnam's Sons, 1973).
11. Karl Jaspers, *The Great Philosophers* (New York: Harcourt Brace, 1957).
12. Dr. Nancy Larrick, *Parents' Guide to Children's Reading* (New York: Doubleday, 1975).
13. Fitzhugh Dodson, Ph.D., *I Wish I Had a Computer That Makes Waffles* (La Jolla, California: Oak Tree Publications, Inc., 1978).